CONTENTS

INTRODUCTION

Of all the animals on earth, the horse is unique on two counts: he has been the most useful to man and, at the same time, has also inspired strong emotions.

It has been said many times that it was the horse that changed the history of the world, not humankind. Without horses, the development and spread of human races, societies and cultures would have taken place much more slowly and, almost certainly, differently. Human leisure and sporting interests would also have been very different and industry could never have developed as we know it. Transport and travel would have been extremely difficult without horses.

Although the horse has always been mainly a working animal (and this includes today's leisure horses), he also inspires love, admiration and wonder in a manner that no mechanical invention can – and, in his own way, he can give a tremendous amount back to us, too.

For most readers of this book, their horse will be a very important part of their lifestyle – a hobby, maybe, but one to which they are seriously committed. Those who do not own a horse or pony can be just as determined to ride and look after a horse, even if only at weekends at a local riding school, because of the physical and mental benefits that riding brings. How else can you experience achievement, intimate contact and affection with another creature, while developing physical fitness, strength and co-ordination, and mental alertness?

Horses are great stress-busters. You have to take your mind off other things and concentrate on the horse, both for his welfare and for the safety of both of you. You have to care for him – and horse chores are very time-consuming – and sacrifice other activities in your life, especially if you have a job as well. All this, though, brings great satisfaction, reward and pride in your horse and in a job well done.

This book is for anyone interested in horses, whether they have a horse of their own or not. It is wide in scope and may broaden your horizons or simply provide absorbing fireside reading. Whichever it is, I do hope you enjoy it.

Essential Horse

Susan McBane

The ultimate guide to caring for and riding your horse

hamlyn

HISTORY OF THE HORSE

Throughout the horse's history as both a wild and, more recently, a domesticated animal, he has been evolving. The first direct ancestor of the horse was a fox-sized, tropical swamp and forest dweller, which then passed through various developmental stages, becoming larger, faster and stronger. He gradually adapted from eating leaves (which horses still sometimes do) and hiding from danger, to eating tough grasses and running away. The final stage of his evolution so far has been as a companion and work-mate to humans – a strange liaison when you consider that we are more predator than prey, with a very different mind-set to that of the horse.

How horses evolved

Although the earliest recognized horse ancestor is known to have existed about 50 million years ago, the modern horse has been domesticated for only about one ten-thousandth of that time – little more than 5,000 years. Horses have been an established type, with firmly ingrained traits, for millions of years more than humans, yet we expect them to fit into our kind of lifestyle almost without question.

The first 'horse'

The so-called 'Dawn Horse', *Hyracotherium*, also known as *Eohippus*, appeared roughly 55 million years ago at the start of the Eocene epoch in what is now North America, when land was mainly swampy, tropical forest.

Hyracotherium was about the size of a fox, with a rounded back. Its small teeth were suitable for browsing – eating leaves and fruits from trees and bushes. It had four hooved toes on its front feet and three on the back, with a central pad as on a dog's paw. It was probably timid and solitary, escaping predators by hiding in undergrowth to evade them rather than running away. Its coat was probably mottled and/or striped, which provided camouflage in the dappled forest light.

This horse's stocky body and copious hair indicate that some of his ancestors evolved in a fairly cold part of the planet.

A horse for all climates

Early equines developed characteristics to suit the region in which they evolved. Those in cold climates developed thicker skin, longer, tougher coats, thick manes and tails, large heads to warm the cold air going in, chunky bodies to help keep in the heat and shorter necks for the same reason. Those in hot regions developed fine skin and coats, fine, sparse mane and tail hair, smaller heads, and longer legs to facilitate air circulation around their bodies.

Fewer toes – bigger teeth

Down the ages, the climate of the earth changed and swamps dwindled to tropical bands, with grasslands taking over in more temperate zones. Over time, and through various ancestral types of horse, the number of toes dwindled to one that was better able to cope with the drier, firmer and more open ground. The teeth became bigger and stronger to grind up the tougher new vegetation – the grasses. The animal became bigger and more like today's horses.

These members of the *Equus* family had specialized, tough running hooves, a longer neck, and a longer, heavier skull than their forebears to hold strong, grazing teeth and the muscles to power big jaws. About the height of a small pony, they would have had all the instincts of modern

Wild types today

All free-living horses are now described as feral, because of human interference with their breeding and distribution. The Przewalski horse (Taki being the local Mongolian name for it), named after the Polish explorer who discovered it, has been reintroduced to its former habitat in Eurasia. It is the purest and nearest thing we have now to a wild, ancestral type and is a cold-climate type. In the wild forests of Poland, the Tarpan, a finer pony type, has been largely 'reconstituted' from its descendants and roams free.

The Przewalski horse is a primitive, cold-climate type of horse.

The horse's love of exercise and speed fits in with its need, as a prey animal, to be able to gallop away from danger.

equines. The *Equus* species we know today – horses, asses and onagers, and zebras – finally emerged about one million years ago.

Spread of horse types

For millions of years, Europe and Asia were linked to North America by land where the Bering Straits (off Alaska) are today. During the Eocene, horse ancestors migrated continually over the Bering land bridge to Asia and Europe. From about three million years ago, there was a huge migration from North America of *Equus* itself, and it became abundant in both New and Old Worlds.

Two momentous events occurred just before the end of the Pleistocene: the arrival of humans in the Americas about 15,000 years ago, followed by the disappearance of the horse from its birthplace, for reasons that are still not clear. By then, the land bridges over which *Equus* had migrated were below sea level. The Americas were not repopulated with horses until the conquistadors arrived in the late 15th century. *Equus* flourished in Eurasia and Africa, however, evolving into horses in Asia and Europe, asses in Africa and Asia, onagers in Asia around present-day Iran and Iraq, and zebras in Africa.

Domestication of the horse

The impact of the domestication of the horse on human society must have been as profound as that of the invention of the steam engine. It probably happened in more than one region of Asia about 5,000–6,000 years ago. The increased mobility provided by the horse enabled previously undreamed-of human expansion. The horse's use in warfare and transport had the effect of transforming the world.

Checklist
- ✓ human meets horse
- ✓ early horsemanship
- ✓ riding and driving
- ✓ training horse relatives
- ✓ effects of domestication

How could it have happened?

Humankind's first contact with the horse would have been as an animal for hunting to eat, like many others.

Wild horses, particularly as foals, can be captured and tamed, and then ridden, harnessed, slaughtered and even eaten without being domesticated. Aboriginal peoples tame all kinds of wild animals to keep as pets and this could have been the case with horses, at least from the time of the earliest anatomically modern humans. When the need arose, taming would probably have been the first step towards domestication.

Close cousins

It is known that asses, onagers and zebras were all brought into the domestication efforts, but only horses, ponies and asses have proved temperamentally suited to working for man. Onagers apparently gratuitously bit and kicked – but as they were controlled by a nose-ring, like cattle, which must have been extremely painful, perhaps this is not terribly surprising!

Recently, British ethologist Dr Marthe Kiley-Worthington and some colleagues captured a wild African zebra and both tamed and trained it like a horse with, apparently, no particular difficulty. In 19th-century England, there was a private coach and four – zebras, not horses – in regular use around London, and one redoubtable English lady hunted riding a zebra.

Early captives would have been restrained in pens or corrals and very gradually accustomed to human pressures such as catching, restraint and tying up, not simply to petting and feeding. Essentially nervous, horses that resisted would have experienced rougher methods of handling, which still exist in some countries today. Tethering would have been introduced fairly soon as a convenient way of keeping horses nearby, and herd size would have been increased by tethering an in-season mare where a wild stallion could approach and mate with her, another practice that probably continues around some feral equines today.

Which came first – riding or driving?

Experts still disagree on this and propose a variety of theories. Probably it would be easier to sit on horses or, at least, start to use them as pack animals.

Early domesticated horses would have been used not only for meat but also for their hide, blood, hair and milk. The constant handling involved in some of these activities would have familiarized them with humans to the extent that when, perhaps, children were playing near them, they lay across them and the horses did not really object. On the move, maybe a traveller rested his pack on a horse's back, or a child or aged or infirm person would be placed on a horse for ease of travel, and things developed from there.

As for driving, the travois – a frame of two trailing poles fixed on each side of a simple harness and filled in with hide or woven twigs – was an early invention. Sledges developed in colder climes and then wheeled vehicles, which would eventually change the world forever.

Effects of domestication

Almost any veterinary surgeon or equine scientist will confirm that most of the diseases from which domesticated horses and ponies suffer are not seen in feral equines. Diseases such as laminitis, 'broken wind' (Recurrent Airway Obstruction), azoturia and 'tying up', navicular disease and colic (see pages 184–185) are all caused by management inappropriate to the individual horse suffering from them.

As equine research continues apace, we learn more and more about how to manage horses more suitably, from both

Above Heavy draught horses, like this one, are still used in some countries for farming, transport and logging.
Below Herding cattle is one of the oldest jobs of the ridden horse. The modern vehicles now so often used are not as efficient or helpful.

a mental and a physical point of view. This is not only more humane but also economically advantageous. Domestication will continue because of our attraction to the horse, but we should ensure that it is largely to the horse's advantage, not his detriment.

Did you know ...?

Apart from Antarctica, Australasia is the only continent with no native or indigenous horses. It split off from the world's land mass much earlier than other continents, and horses had not reached there at that time.

However, in many areas it has provided an ideal environment for equine species to flourish, both ferally and in domestication. Horses were first taken to Australasia by settlers in the 18th century, and the Australian Brumby, or feral, horse is now world famous, New Zealand's Kaimanawa horse a little less so.

The development of breeds

Soon after appreciating the usefulness of horses, humans realized that certain types were better at particular tasks than others – some were good for riding, some for harness work, some were fast and others slow but strong. As travel became easier, people saw different types of horse in other regions with different qualities from their own.

Checklist

✓ horse trading
✓ natural evolution of types
✓ breeding desirable qualities
✓ two extremes: racing and draught

Travel and trade

Travelling demands different types of horse according to how you want to travel. Early peoples often migrated along with the herds of other animals, such as reindeer and cattle, on which they depended for food and other goods. Often, they took not only themselves but also their homes and chattels as well. Those in charge of the party needed fast horses with stamina for riding ahead and scouting; others, probably guards, would have had slower horses, while the horses needed for pulling transport vehicles would have been heavier and very strong.

Peoples travelling near or across their borders or along accepted trade routes bartered not only goods and foods but also horses and other animals. This was one way in which desired equine characteristics were obtained for breeding into the existing stock of a tribe or family.

Natural horse types

Nature created various equines to suit the different climatic conditions.

• Desert animals in general are fine-skinned with short, fine body coats and mane and tail hair. Such horses, still known as hot-bloods, were generally very alert, possibly temperamental, sensitive and easily upset. Today, we think of Thoroughbreds, Arabs, Akhal-Tekes, Caspians and similar breeds.

• Animals evolving in tundras and steppes are designed to withstand bitter cold, blizzards and poor grazing, and are

The Shetland Pony is a classic north European indigenous type, well able to bear the rigours of a cold, windswept landscape.

know as cold-bloods. Their thicker skin, chunkier bodies and longer, coarser body coats and mane and tail hair help to keep heat within the body. They have more placid temperaments and are generally not so excitable. The Przewalski horse is one of these, as are the Shetland, the Norwegian Fjord, the Icelandic and the Shire.

These 'pure' types were readily mixed and matched by early peoples and today there are well over 300 distinct breeds around the world.

Custom-made qualities

It would not take a perceptive horseperson very long to learn how to mate particular individuals to produce an animal that they hoped would combine the characteristics of each parent. Experience, however, would show that it is not that straightforward, and the breeder would learn which

horses, male or female, produced offspring that always took after them and which did not.

In this way, different characteristics required by people became predictable, and families or strains of horses with desired traits were established – gallopers, jumpers, draught horses for transport, chariot horses for war and racing, small animals for children, steady ones for the old and infirm, and so on.

One of the earliest recorded specific types of horse – which today we would probably call a breed – was the Heavenly Horse of China, but the Arab peoples, particularly the Bedouin, took breeding to a fine art. Breeds with stud books and written records are probably only 200 or, at most, 300 years old. Before that, pedigrees were handed down by word of mouth and perhaps could not always be relied upon!

Opposite ends of the scale

Of all the man-made breeds, probably the two most widely divergent types are the Thoroughbred and the Shire. Both English breeds, their characteristics and their genes have spread around the world and influenced many other breeds.

• The Thoroughbred was developed exclusively for speed in racing, to the exclusion of all other qualities. The breed in general is noted for an excitable temperament, physical sensitivity, rather poor feet, and (in some bloodlines) 'burning out' from nervous energy and worrying, but also for great courage under pressure. (See also pages 166–167.)

Heavily muscled horses such as the Ardennais (above) and the Shire love to gallop and play, but are generally more placid than hot-bloods.

• The Shire hails from the Midlands of England. The breed was developed as an extremely strong horse for heavy farm work and pulling heavy vehicles in other industries, working singly, in pairs or in teams. It is large, massively muscled with a large, Roman-nosed head, short, thick neck, and much hair or 'feather' on the lower legs and around large, dinnerplate-sized feet. These horses can work all day at slow gaits and are still used for short-haul deliveries.

Hot-blooded horses such as Thoroughbreds show their characters and speed at an early age, with their peers in their paddocks.

Riding through history

No other animal has a back so suitable for sitting on. Since not all horses are comfortable to ride bareback, saddles developed over the centuries. Animal skins were used first (we still use them today) and possibly padded clothing for the rider, then a padded framework was devised. Once the stirrup appeared, with its added security, riding was transformed.

Checklist
✓ horses for herdsmen
✓ the changing war horse
✓ working horses

Horses for herding

Early equestrian peoples probably lived in today's Middle East, but written records (often on clay tablets) about how they rode are few. Today, the peoples of the northern and eastern Asian steppes – Russia and farther east – are probably our earliest 'living record' of how people used and rode their horses. For instance, for the Kabardin herdsmen of the Caucasus mountains in eastern Europe, their renowned breed of horse is still central to their lives.

Any people using horses for herding spent long hours in the saddle, so the eventual development of a comfortable saddle, and a bridle and bit that effectively controlled the horse, was crucial. The herders of Hungary, the Csikos, were also of this type and are still formidable riders, horse tamers and trainers.

The war horse

However, it was the use of the horse in war that changed the course of world history. For a thousand years or more, horses were used to carry warriors and their weapons to the site of the battle, where they dismounted and fought on foot.

Saddles with stirrups make long hours in the saddle much more comfortable and secure.

Tack fact

Stirrups were probably not invented until around 2,000 years ago, although expert opinion differs on this. Initially they were rawhide loops, developing to wood and then metal. Today's stainless steel stirrups are the strongest there have ever been, although new synthetic materials are now both very strong and light, too. Light stirrups, though, are harder to regain in motion if you 'lose' them, as they fly around with the horse's movement.

Racing Thoroughbreds, a multi-billion dollar industry, exploits the breed's speed and courage.

Some of the first truly mounted warriors were the Assyrian archers from around present-day Iraq and the River Tigris. They sat, without saddles, towards the back of their horses with their legs raised high, and for stability used short, stiffened reins that were easy to seize quickly. Their favoured mount was of the type that today would be recognized as the Turcoman and Akhal-Teke from the Asian steppes. Tough, enduring and fast, they are probably the ancestors of the Arabian and Thoroughbred and are still bred today.

Early art shows warriors sitting on the croups of animals no taller than small ponies, and although this position allowed the horses to bear their weight directly over a strong part of the body, it was not a position from which a rider had much control. Around the 5th century BC, the first academic approach to riding that we know of was put forward by the Greek cavalry commander Xenophon. His soldiers rode without stirrups and in a forward-type seat.

As armour was developed, the horses needed to be bigger and stronger to carry both it and the rider. Indeed, the horses themselves were often armoured as well. However, the myth that the English Shire horse is the descendant of the 'great' war horse of the Middle Ages is just that. Contemporary armour for horse and man, of which much remains, shows that the horses were of strong cob type of a maximum height of 15 hands (152 cm) – and at the time that was big. Horses continued to play a role in warfare, becoming taller but finer and faster as armour disappeared and gunfire developed.

Riding today for work and pleasure

The horse is certainly used more today for leisure pursuits than for what we regard as work. However, to the horse it is all the same. In nearly every country some horses are still used for traditional work, such as harness both heavy and light, and in some less developed countries they are more important than motorized vehicles and machines.

For some jobs – mounted police and rangers, logging in difficult terrain, short-haul deliveries such as for breweries, cattle herding and others – the horse is far more practical and economical than his mechanized equivalent. Many countries also still maintain horses for ceremonial and prestige jobs, and they add immeasurably to the image of those places.

Did you know ...?

Horses were used for pack work and transport during the early years of World War II, and are still used for that purpose in war today in more remote areas of the world.

Riding styles around the world

It seems easy to get on a horse and just sit there, but from this basic, natural seat many different riding styles have developed. Probably the most stunning example of man learning to ride comes from the Native Americans. They had never seen a horse before the arrival of the conquistadors, yet they became, according to General Custer, 'the finest light cavalry in the world'.

Early riders

The eastern Asians – Mongols, Japanese, Turcomans and so on – often rode (and still ride) with short stirrups and sometimes rely heavily on the reins for control and balance. However, in warfare some were famed for standing up in their stirrups at a flat-out gallop, guiding the horse with their knees, and using both hands to fight with bow and arrow, lance and sword.

Civilizations such as the Romans and Greeks rode initially without stirrups and – judging by the distressed demeanour of the famous statues of horses in the Piazza San Marco in Venice and those carved in relief around the Parthenon frieze – were very heavy-handed. Xenophon (see pages 16–17) sought to correct this, and the style of riding we now call 'classical' derives from his teachings.

Knights in shining armour

The Middle Ages produced the 'airs above the ground' (controlled leaps) of High School riding, which were based on war manoeuvres aimed at protecting the rider or

Did you know ...?

The first known books on horses and riding are still available for us all to learn from today. They were written in the era of classical Greece nearly 2,500 years ago by the Greek cavalry commander Xenophon. Entitled *Hippike* and *Hipparchikos*, today they appear as one volume called *The Art of Horsemanship*. The book has been translated into many languages and still has much to teach us.

The Western seat

This seat was developed from the classical seat specifically for riders herding cattle, and is based on that used in Iberia and southern France for managing the aggressive black cattle of the region. Taken to the Americas with Iberian horses by the conquistadors, lightness is very much the aim: there is a long stirrup and little or no contact with the bit in the trained horse, under a skilled rider.

unseating or killing opponents. The influence of the mounted knights persisted until the 14th century, when the new, more powerful bows and arrows forced them to encase themselves and their necessarily larger, heavier mounts in sheet armour rather than chain mail, and they became cumbersome sitting targets.

Equitation as an art form

Riding was first recognized as an art form in the Renaissance period, when no nobleman's education was considered complete until he had acquired an appreciation of equitation. Elegant Baroque riding halls sprang up all over Europe to house the stately carousels (musical rides) and displays performed by these aristocrats.

However, despite the rediscovery of Xenophon's texts, there was much brutality in training until an enlightened, more humane approach to horsemanship spread across Europe, due particularly to the influence of François Robichon de la Guérinière (1688–1751). His humane and understanding influence, and his development of the shoulder-in – in which the horse carries himself at an angle to the direction of movement – as a suppling exercise, changed the course of classical equitation. His teachings form the foundation of modern schooling methods.

The American saddle seat

Not everyone followed de la Guérinière's teachings, and a European method upon which the American saddle seat is based continued in some quarters and was taken to the New World by European settlers. Usually, in this seat the rider is (by classical tenets) seated behind the horse's centre of balance with the legs forward. The head of the horse is required to be carried high and his feet are lengthened to create a high lifting motion of the legs. Some proponents of this style are, apparently, now moving more towards classical principles.

Right The 'forward seat' for jumping and galloping made life much easier for horse and rider than the old, unbalanced, vertical position. Below Skilled Western riding is a pure form of classical riding.

Hunting and jumping

The fast, galloping sport of foxhunting developed in England and Ireland during the 18th century, turning these riders away from classical riding in an arena towards that sport, and to racing across country on their superlative Thoroughbred horses.

Initially, the seats used for hunting and racing were still upright with long stirrups, but American jockey Tod Sloane (1874–1933) popularized the 'monkey-up-a-stick' seat for racing, with very short stirrups and the rider's body over the horse's shoulders, that is still used today.

Italian cavalry officer Federico Caprilli (1868–1907) revolutionized jumping and cross-country riding with his balanced 'forward seat'. Here the rider takes most weight in the stirrups, bends forward from the hip joints with a flat back and positions the upper body over the horse's shoulders in order to remain more easily over the horse's centre of gravity during jumping and galloping across uneven terrain. Today, however, a more upright seat between jumps is considered safer.

For dressage and schooling on the flat (not over jumps), the classical seat is still the best, with its basis on the vertical upper body and in the seat and legs rather than the hands, but not all riders follow this in its pure form.

The working horse

Even today, a century after the invention of the internal combustion engine and two centuries after steam was first harnessed as an energy source, the power of an engine is still often measured in 'horse power'. Perhaps this is not so surprising, for until the latter years of the 19th century, horse power was virtually the only motive power available.

The pack horse

The horse's first job was probably that of pack animal, and in prehistoric times he carried anything from baskets of peat to the carcasses of game animals. Several thousand years later, trappers in newly settled America were using the same means to take their furs to the trading posts, while to this day Shetland ponies carry peat for fuel to the crofts in the Scottish Highlands and the Highland pony himself still carries deer carcasses down from the hill.

Horse-drawn vehicles

Early harness used the yoke, allowing the horse to pull more weight than he could carry. The chariot came next and was mainly used for racing, for war and for transporting eminent people. In the Middle Ages, the heavy coaches demanded strong, powerful horses to pull huge weights over (or through) routes axle-deep in mud, but as roads improved there appeared lighter and, from the 18th century, extremely elegant carriages, drawn by equally elegant horses.

18th-century advances

As roads improved and sprung suspensions were invented, travelling fairly fast over long distances by coach and carriage became feasible. In the UK, the first Royal Mail coaches appeared in 1784. This was also the age of the canals, along which big horses towed heavily laden barges for great distances inland.

The 19th century

The 19th century is probably best known for opening up the Wild West of America, with its cow ponies, covered wagons, Texas rangers and the Pony Express. Cities all over the western world were packed with horses and the traffic jam, horse-style, was common.

Horses were used for almost every job imaginable, and were invaluable for the new emergency services and police forces. Fast roadsters, for which Norfolk, England, was particularly famous, became desired worldwide for fast, long-distance transport.

Two heavy horses take part in a ploughing competition. Horses plough much deeper than most tractors and fertilize the land as they go.

Horses were often very badly treated at this time. Anna Sewell's novel *Black Beauty* drew attention to their plight, and helped to stimulate a movement towards improving equine welfare.

The horse in agriculture

The horse retained his stronghold on farms in the western hemisphere until the 20th century, when motorized tractors took over. In eastern Europe and many Asian countries, however, horse-drawn vehicles and ploughs have always been vital to agriculture.

Today, even in the west, heavy horses can be seen working in the fields and delivering barrels of beer to inns near their stables. In Finland, for example, there are an estimated 150,000 horses working on farms and in forests.

Logging is one industry that in many areas could barely survive without horses. They can go into places where vehicles cannot, and can learn to work virtually alone, so saving on manpower.

The Royal Canadian Mounted Police display team gives displays all over the world, thrilling the crowds with the harmony and teamwork they exhibit.

Modern equine roles

Around the middle of the 20th century there was an explosion in the popularity of riding as a leisure pursuit. The most popular equestrian sports worldwide are showjumping, dressage, eventing, polo, carriage driving, hunting and rodeo in some countries, showing, reining, racing both under saddle and in harness, and endurance riding. However, not everyone wants to compete – many just love riding at a riding school as a weekend relaxation, although more and more people keep their own horses in livery stables.

Ceremonial horses are still a much-valued part of society in some countries, and many police forces admit that they could not fulfil certain aspects of their role so effectively without their mounted officers.

ANATOMY, PHYSIOLOGY

Horses in our society are nearly always athletic animals, used for athletic pursuits. They must be strong, and certainly need to be ridden and managed with a basic, working understanding of how they are constructed and how they function, both mentally and physically. Even breeding animals, which are often never ridden, need to be strong and healthy. If you know how your horse's mind and body work, you will be able to care for him properly and ride him considerately. This does not mean that you won't be able to do demanding work with him (provided he is fit enough to do it) but it does mean that you will minimize his chance of injury and also make it very unlikely that behaviour problems will arise.

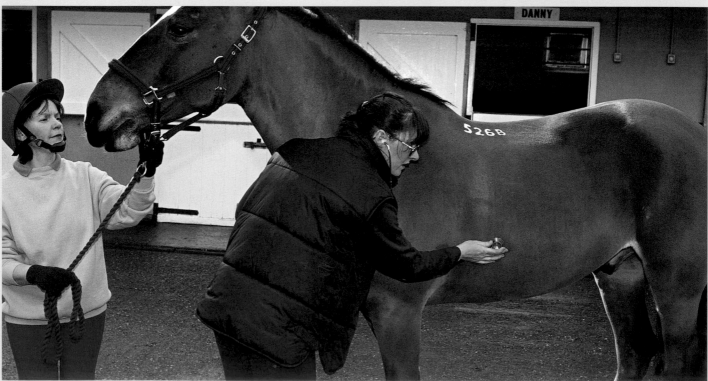

AND BEHAVIOUR

The horse's body

Most people who love horses think they are beautiful animals. When healthy, they are strong, fast and agile but they do suffer from injury, disease and ageing. Horses are specialized grazing, running prey animals. Most large animals are not fast and athletic, and it is this combination of size and speed that makes the horse able to live the life nature ordained for him.

Checklist
✓ the body's framework
✓ ligaments, muscles and tendons
✓ complex hooves
✓ specialized teeth
✓ energy-efficient design

Skeleton

The skeleton is the framework around which the horse's body is constructed. It protects his vital organs and enables him to move. Minerals are stored in the bones, and blood cells are made in the bone marrow.

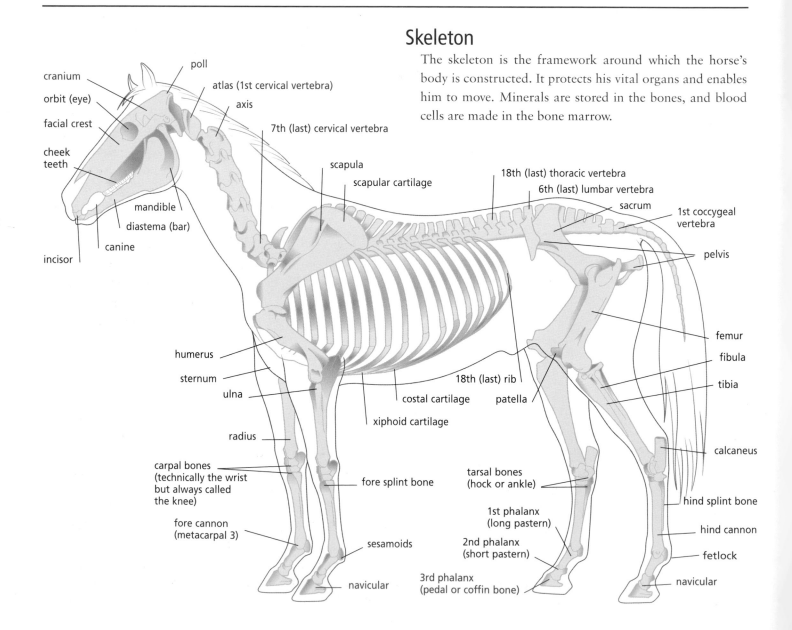

poll
cranium
atlas (1st cervical vertebra)
orbit (eye)
axis
facial crest
7th (last) cervical vertebra
cheek teeth
scapula
scapular cartilage
18th (last) thoracic vertebra
6th (last) lumbar vertebra
sacrum
1st coccygeal vertebra
mandible
diastema (bar)
canine
pelvis
incisor
femur
humerus
fibula
sternum
tibia
ulna
18th (last) rib
patella
costal cartilage
radius
xiphoid cartilage
calcaneus
carpal bones (technically the wrist but always called the knee)
tarsal bones (hock or ankle)
fore splint bone
hind splint bone
fore cannon (metacarpal 3)
1st phalanx (long pastern)
hind cannon
2nd phalanx (short pastern)
fetlock
sesamoids
3rd phalanx (pedal or coffin bone)
navicular
navicular

Bone consists partly of fibrous protein tissue and partly of minerals (calcium, phosphorus and some magnesium). The ends of bones are covered by gristly cartilage for protection. Bone is far from being a fixed, rigid material, and is able to respond to injury and the stresses of work by repairing and strengthening itself. It also contains channels for the passage of blood and lymph vessels, and nerves, all of which maintain the bone.

Ligaments

These are tough sheets, bands or cords of fibrous tissue that 'bind' the bones together at joints. They have a good nerve supply so are very sensitive, but have a poor blood supply which means they can take a long time to recover from injury.

Muscles and tendons

Muscles responsible for moving the skeleton are attached to a bone at one end and to a different bone at the other via a tendon. This is a slightly elastic, tough cord of adapted muscle tissue. The two bones are linked by a joint.

When the muscle shortens or contracts it pulls on the tendon, which forces the bone to which it is attached to move, either flexing or extending the joint.

Muscles are very copiously supplied with blood, other fluid and nerves: they are therefore very sensitive and very painful when injured, but heal relatively quickly. Tendons are sensitive but not well supplied with blood, so, like ligaments, can take a long time to heal.

Energy savers

• The horse has no muscles in his lower legs. Muscle tissue contains a lot of fluid and so is heavy. The horse's feet are also light. This combined lightness of the lower leg enables the horse to use less energy to move it and to keep going – essential qualities in an animal evolved to run for his life away from predators.

• The tendons in the legs have a slight elastic quality. When weight is put on them they stretch a little, then as the weight is relieved they recoil, giving the horse a boost in his stride that requires no energy-consuming effort from him.

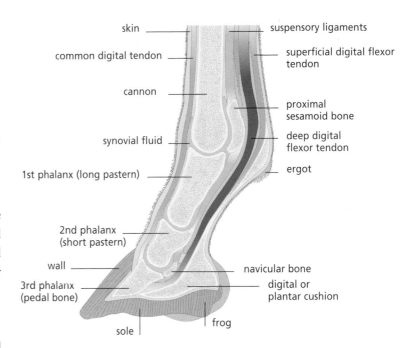

skin — suspensory ligaments — common digital tendon — superficial digital flexor tendon — cannon — proximal sesamoid bone — synovial fluid — deep digital flexor tendon — 1st phalanx (long pastern) — ergot — 2nd phalanx (short pastern) — wall — navicular bone — 3rd phalanx (pedal bone) — digital or plantar cushion — sole — frog

Feet

The legs obviously end in the feet, or hooves, which are complex structures of bone, horn, sensitive tissue, fibrous cushioning tissue, blood and nerves. The horn that forms the wall of the hoof that we can see grows down from the ridge at the top of the wall, called the coronet, taking about a year to grow from coronet to ground at the toe depending on individual growth rate and diet.

Underneath, the hoof is uneven for 'grip' (like the tread on walking boots). In the middle is the frog, a structure made from horn of a rubbery consistency. The frog, plus the expansion and contraction of the heels with each step, helps to pump the blood around the foot and lower leg. (See also pages 74–75.)

Teeth

The horse has a relatively large head in order to accommodate the large, strong teeth that are needed to grind up his tough natural food – grass. Like other mammals, horses have milk and permanent teeth.

The front teeth, or incisors, are for tearing off grass, and the back, or cheek teeth – the premolars and molars – are for grinding it up. Male horses (stallions and geldings), and very occasionally females (mares), also have tushes, or canine teeth, just behind the incisors.

The space on the jawbones between the front and back teeth is where the bit lies. This area of the lower jaw is called the 'bars' and, conveniently for us, there are no teeth here.

Heart and lungs

Together, the heart and lungs provide the body's transport system for delivery of nutrients, hormones, oxygen and medicines, and removal of waste and toxic products, some of which are created during metabolism. The horse's circulatory system is, relatively, much more efficient than ours, not surprising in a natural athlete, but his lungs are sensitive, making him prone to diseases and allergies in domestication.

Heart

The heart is a muscular organ with four hollow chambers: the left and right atriums, or upper chambers, and the left and right ventricles, or lower chambers. The walls are made up of specialized muscle, which is electrically stimulated to contract, pumping blood through the heart and around the body. Valves between the chambers of the heart prevent the blood from flowing backwards when the chambers contract. The heart is divided from top to bottom by a muscular wall.

Blood enters and leaves the heart via arteries, which carry blood away from the heart, and veins, which carry it to the heart. The vessels gradually reduce in size until they mesh in an extensive, complicated network of microscopic tubes (capillaries) almost all over the body, through the walls of which substances pass to and from the body tissues.

Blood

Blood consists of plasma, cells and platelets.
Plasma is composed of serum, a fluid that is mainly water plus some nutrients, and fibrinogen, a protein that aids blood clotting to help repair injuries.

Did you know ...?

The horse's body makes over 35 million red blood cells every day. These can be stored in a reservoir called the spleen, which, if stimulated by the hormone adrenalin, can release extra cells when extra oxygen is needed such as during hard work. The spleen also makes lymphocytes.

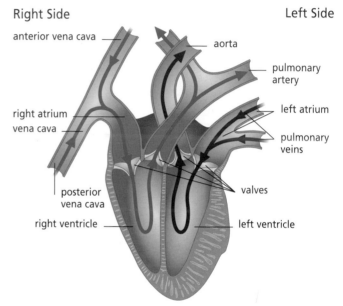

Right Side   Left Side

anterior vena cava
aorta
pulmonary artery
right atrium
vena cava
left atrium
pulmonary veins
posterior vena cava
valves
right ventricle
left ventricle

The blue line represents deoxygenated blood flowing from the body to the lungs; the red is oxygenated blood flowing from the lungs back to the body.

Blood cells are mainly red and white. The red cells contain haemoglobin, an iron-containing pigment that can pick up and transport the oxygen breathed into the lungs. In the capillary network, the oxygen passes out to the tissues and carbon dioxide passes in (called 'gaseous exchange'), to be dissolved in the plasma. Back in the lungs, the carbon dioxide is breathed out. The white cells, of five types, repair dead and damaged tissue and fight disease.
Platelets are cell fragments that congregate at injury sites and assist fibrinogen to clot blood and form a temporary repair until new tissue is made.

Lymph

Lymph is another fluid consisting of water, protein, fat and some white cells called lymphocytes. It helps to fight disease and nourishes tissues that have no blood supply such as the

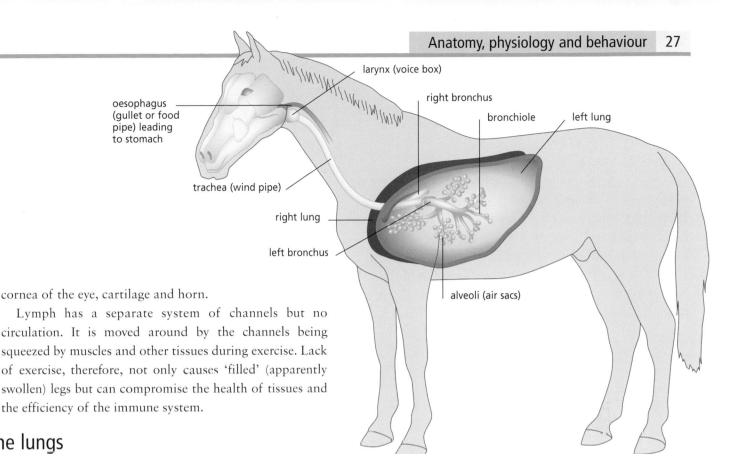

larynx (voice box)

right bronchus

bronchiole

left lung

oesophagus (gullet or food pipe) leading to stomach

trachea (wind pipe)

right lung

left bronchus

alveoli (air sacs)

The lungs and heart fill the thorax, or chest cavity, and are separated from the abdominal contents by a strong, dome-shaped muscle called the diaphragm.

cornea of the eye, cartilage and horn.

Lymph has a separate system of channels but no circulation. It is moved around by the channels being squeezed by muscles and other tissues during exercise. Lack of exercise, therefore, not only causes 'filled' (apparently swollen) legs but can compromise the health of tissues and the efficiency of the immune system.

The lungs

Oxygen is supplied to the horse's body via the respiratory system. Air is drawn through the nose, past the larynx, or voicebox, and into the trachea, or windpipe. The trachea passes into the thorax, or chest, and into the lungs.

At this point it divides into two smaller tubes (left and right to the left and right lungs) called bronchi, and these divide into even smaller ones called bronchioles. At the ends of the bronchioles are alveoli, tiny air sacs that look like hollow bunches of grapes, surrounded by capillaries. Here, carbon dioxide passes out of the blood and oxygen passes in.

Small particles of debris often enter the respiratory system, but the cells lining the nasal passages, trachea and bronchi produce mucus, which helps to trap debris and airborne contaminants. There are also small hair-like projections called cilia, which, by means of wave-like movement towards the nostrils, help to move the debris out of the lungs so that it can be coughed up.

Horses' respiratory systems are adversely affected by dust – bedding, forage, dry feeds, grooming the horse in his stable, working in an indoor riding school or even a dusty outdoor arena all challenge the airways. Air pollution from, say, exhaust fumes and ammonia from decomposing urine and dirty, damp bedding commonly irritate the sensitive linings of the lungs as well.

Keeping the lungs healthy

- Groom your horse outdoors whenever possible.
- Use non-dusty bedding and feed.
- Dampen his feed slightly if it is not moist already.
- Do not stable your horse near a busy road or the yard's car park.
- Site the car park and muck heap downwind from the stables.
- Turn your horse out in his field in the fresh air and ride him out as much as you reasonably can.
- Try a herbal supplement made for breathing problems, if your horse is affected.

The nervous and endocrine systems

Communication from both within and outside the body is essential to life and survival. The horse's body needs information about what is happening outside, affecting his comfort and safety, and inside, affecting his optimal functioning. These jobs are performed by the nervous and endocrine (hormonal) systems. They give the horse his lightning-quick reactions to external stimuli while controlling his inner environment as well.

Checklist
✓ how nerves work
✓ the body's messengers
✓ over-riding messages
✓ preparing for action – and inaction
✓ hormones: controlling function and behaviour
✓ hormonal imbalances

The nervous system

The horse's main control centre is his central nervous system (CNS). This is composed of the brain and the spinal cord, which runs from the brain and continues down inside the backbone. There is also the peripheral nervous system (PNS), an extremely complex network of nerves running out from the spinal cord through grooves or spaces between the vertebrae, which are the bones that make up the load-bearing backbone.

If the horse feels something unpleasant such as pain or irritation, nerves in the PNS called sensory nerves sense this and send electrical messages to the CNS. The CNS assesses these messages and sends a reply back down the motor (movement) nerves in the PNS to do something about it, such as move away from the pain, scratch an itch and so on.

When excess heat is detected, such as on a hot day or in a muggy stable or horsebox, the reaction is to widen blood vessels near the skin surface and bring more heat-carrying blood to the skin, from where the excess heat can escape into the environment. The coat will be told to flatten and the sweat glands to give out heat-containing sweat to evaporate away the excess body heat. All this is reversed when the horse feels cold.

Action and inaction

There is also a system called the autonomic nervous system, which works without conscious control, which itself has two parts – the sympathetic system, which prepares the body for action by, for example, warning the horse of danger or prompting him to roll in the mud, and the parasympathetic system, which prepares him for relaxation, eating and sleeping.

Frequently asked question

 I know that horses are sensitive and can, for example, feel a fly landing on their skin. Why is it, then, that my horse often ignores my leg signals (aids) when I know very well that he can feel them?

 This is because, in many circumstances, a horse can decide for himself whether or not to respond to stimuli like leg aids or a whip, or whether to over-ride what his internal messages are telling him. In particular, riders who squeeze or kick with their legs at every stride (some instructors even teach people to do this) are actually 'wearing out' the horse's response capability. The aids become like 'white noise' – they are always there and become part of the furniture, part of being ridden, so the horse ignores them.

The endocrine system

The endocrine system is concerned with the production and distribution of hormones. It works with the nervous system but more slowly and its effects are longer-lasting, sometimes considerably so.

The endocrine system consists of glands found at various points in the horse's body, which produce chemical messengers, or hormones, that circulate in the blood. These control the horse's functioning and emotions and, therefore, his behaviour. The system also controls functions such as digestion, lactation, excretion, the rate of growth and development, ageing and very many others – in effect, the whole of life's processes. Hormonal imbalances can be mild or severe and, in extreme cases, life-threatening.

The main gland is the pituitary, situated just below the brain, which controls other glands and is itself controlled by part of the brain called the hypothalamus, which also secretes various hormones. Two more important glands are the adrenal glands sited very near the kidneys, which secrete the hormone adrenalin. This is released when a horse is frightened or angry and is part of the famous 'flight or fight' response.

Mares have a hormonally controlled breeding cycle ('season' or oestrus) running over about 21 days. There is also an annual cycle affecting both mares and stallions, which explains why they are interested in breeding in spring, summer and autumn but not in winter. The two hormones most concerned with their distracted and excitable behaviour at these times are testosterone in stallions and oestrogen in mares.

Hormones make a mare feel maternal and the foal feel the need of his dam. Gradually, this mutual need lessens but the bond will remain.

Male horses often play-fight quite aggressively, mostly in spring and early summer when, in the wild, they would be maintaining harems.

Equine fact

It is estimated that over three-quarters of geldings (castrated male horses) retain some stallion characteristics, particularly if they were gelded some time after puberty and especially if they had already served mares.
This is why the behaviour of some geldings, not just stallions and mares, changes from early spring onwards when the 'breeding' hormones start circulating in their blood.

Skin, hair and horn

Together, skin, hair and horn cover and protect most of the horse except the eyes, which have eyelids and eyelashes instead. The condition of skin, hair and horn is a good indicator of health, and they are kept healthy by a diet balanced in nutrients, natural exposure to weather and the mutual grooming of herd mates, who groom each other with muzzles and teeth. They tend their own skin by rolling and rubbing.

Checklist
✓ the sensitive skin
✓ daylength and coat changes
✓ functions of the mane and tail
✓ the horse's 'antennae'
✓ horn and hoof protection
✓ effects of feeding

Skin

The skin is an elastic protector of the sensitive body underneath. It has two main layers: the 'dead' outer layer, or epidermis, and the sensitive under layer, or dermis. When in good health, a horse's skin is usually easily moved over his ribs, and feels loose and elastic. It has no lumps, bumps, swollen areas or obvious soreness, growths, discharging areas or breaks in the skin.

Skin cells are constantly being renewed from inside out, the outer layer forming dead skin cells, which are shed and seen as dandruff in the horse's coat. The hairs have their roots in the dermis but penetrate the epidermis, as is also the case with the sweat glands and their outlets. The capillary network stops short of the epidermis, as do nerves, but this outer layer is very thin which means that the skin remains very sensitive.

The skin is usually thicker over the top half of the body, to help protect against weather, and thinner underneath. The skin on the legs is quite thin but there may be protective 'feather', or long hair.

Fine-coated horses need outdoor clothing in cold, windy or wet weather, but those with thicker coats will be more comfortable without this layer.

Functions of the skin

• Protects the underlying tissues from weather, toxins, pathogens ('germs'), minor injuries and excess moisture or dryness.

• Is important in regulating body temperature.

• Excretes waste products in the sweat.

• Via nerve endings, it senses information in the outside environment such as heat, cold, pressure, irritation and pain.

• Is instrumental in the formation of Vitamin D in the body.

• Lubricates and protects itself and the hair by means of oil (sebaceous) glands.

• Contains the protective colouring agent melanin, which also strengthens the skin to some degree.

This pony has a generous mane and forelock for protection from the cold, and his natural vibrissae, or 'antenna' whiskers, which act as feelers, are clearly visible.

Coat hair

The horse has a short summer coat and a long winter coat, changing from one to the other twice a year, over several weeks, in spring and autumn. Horses that live near the equator, however, have a summer coat all year round, and can breed all year round as well.

Although warmth and good food help in producing a shorter coat, the main factor is the horse's exposure to light. For instance, as soon as the days start to lengthen, the winter coat begins to cast (shed), despite still-cold weather and poor grazing. One of the signs of good health in a horse is a 'lively', glossy coat.

Mane, tail and forelock hair

These do not cast like the body hair, except in a very few breeds such as the Bashkir. They add extra insulation on the neck and between the buttocks where the skin is thin. They are also useful to a limited extent in protecting against insects, but in insect weather horses also need a cool, shady shelter.

Whiskers (vibrissae)

These antennae-like hairs are important to the horse for sensing his immediate environment and some breed societies are now forbidding their removal for showing, which unfortunately is quite common. Those around the eyes help the horse to protect his head, while those around the muzzle help him to find food and other objects when he is foraging.

Horn

Horn is a variation of hair, both being made from a hard, protein substance called keratin. Its job is to protect the sensitive structures inside the foot. Good, balanced feeding is essential for the formation of tough, resilient horn, and also for good skin and hair. If you feed a supplement to improve, say, hoof health, the hair and skin improve as well, and vice versa.

There is a protective, varnish-like layer on the outside of the horn, which should not be rasped off during shoeing. The horn should also not be soaked in ordinary hoof oils as these can adversely affect its moisture balance.

The horse's senses

The horse's senses give him a different perception of the world to ours. They enable him to survive as a grazing, running prey animal living on large tracts of open grassland. The horse's sometimes apparently strange behaviour may be due to him not seeing things as we see them, or be caused by being able to hear and smell things undetectable to us. Understanding this enables us to understand his behaviour better.

Checklist

✔ the horse's world view
✔ acute hearing
✔ all-round vision
✔ the importance of smell
✔ taste and food selection
✔ touch sensitivity

Hearing

The horse's ears move, often independently, in an almost 180-degree arc, efficiently picking up sounds from all around. Most horses become disturbed or distressed in noisy environments.

The horse can hear sounds outside our range. A fairly common phenomenon is that of tonic immobility: the horse, ridden or otherwise, suddenly stops and, quite relaxed, becomes apparently transfixed by some information coming to him that is outside his handler's or rider's perception. The strange thing is that nothing the handler does will persuade the horse to move on. Indeed, he seems oblivious to everything in his immediate environment. Then, suddenly, he will move his attention 'back to earth' and proceed as if nothing had happened. It is most likely that the horse has been listening to something outside our hearing range that fascinates him – probably the sounds of other horses in the distance.

The earth moves

It is commonly believed that horses can feel vibrations in the earth from many metres away, which may warn them of other approaching animals. Their predators in the wild are mainly of the dog and cat families, which move more softly and stealthily. However, Native American trackers commonly used to put an ear close to the ground to listen, or feel, whether or not pursuers were nearby, and perhaps horses are using a similar strategy.

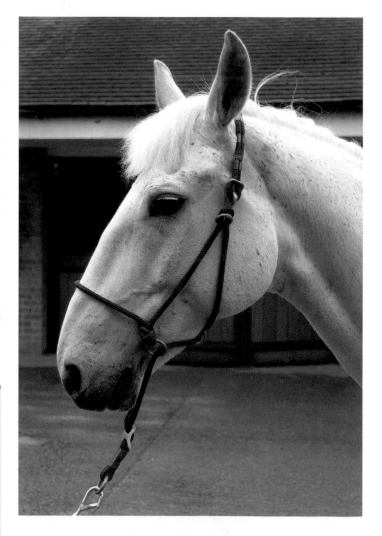

Ears held sideways, like this, generally show relaxation, although this horse clearly has a wary eye on the photographer.

Horses smell everything before taking it into their mouths. Food that feels unfamiliar may not get past their teeth, unlike this green treat.

Sight

The eyes, placed high up on the sides of the head, give the horse virtually all-round vision, with two small blind spots immediately in front and close, and behind. Horses prefer dim light to darkness and research suggests that they have limited colour vision, probably seeing reds and blues very well but other colours less distinctly.

Smell

Strange-smelling foods often put a horse off eating. Horses use smell to identify and bond with one another, in the herd and between mare and foal, as well as with people.

Taste

Taste is linked to smell and is very important in helping a horse to decide what to eat and what to avoid. It is probably an evolutionary tactic and is perhaps why horses do not become ill from eating poisonous plants as often as we might imagine. These usually taste bitter, and horses will experiment with and eat them only when they are very hungry or extremely bored by a poor selection of grasses in their paddock.

Unfortunately, this suspicion of nearly everything, which is so valuable to the horse, can drive his keepers to

Frequently asked question

Q My competition horse often works up a sweat during his work and I try to get him to take electrolytes in his feed or water to replace those lost. Unfortunately, he almost never eats such 'doctored' offerings, which makes me worry about him dehydrating because often he will not drink what I consider to be enough. What can I do?

A Electrolytes (mineral salts) do have a salty taste, which some horses may reject if they are not used to them. Try putting them in a drink of sugar beet water, the sweetness of which may disguise them. You could also make it a practice to put them in his water and feed after a strenuous workout at home during training, to accustom him to them. If these tactics fail, discuss matters with your vet. If your horse does become dehydrated, a veterinary surgeon can administer fluids by nasal tube or, in some cases, intravenous drip.

distraction when trying to get him to eat something that appears to them to be an excellent food for him.

Touch

Nerve endings in the skin detect pressure, pain, irritation, heat and cold. The horse is extremely sensitive to touch and can feel something as light as a fly landing on his side. A piece of bedding trapped between his skin and his rug, for instance, can drive him crazy with discomfort, particularly if he is the fine-skinned type.

The vibrissae (coarse whiskers) around the muzzle and eyes are important 'feelers' for the horse, enabling him to judge distance and texture. When they are removed, the horse sometimes goes off his food and may become temporarily headshy. More enlightened owners leave these whiskers on.

The digestive system

Evolution has not perfected the horse's digestive system. Horses are 'obligate herbivores' – they must eat vegetation, which is bulky and not always very nutritious. Therefore, they must eat a lot of it to obtain their nourishment. The digestive system has a narrow point, the 'pelvic flexure' in the large intestine, which seems prone to blockages – known as impaction colic – caused by their necessarily bulky diet.

Checklist

✓ the system is very sensitive
✓ how the teeth work
✓ horses need roughage
✓ keep cereal grains to a minimum
✓ micro-organisms digest fibre
✓ sudden changes in diet can trigger colic

Teeth

Despite dietary changes, the horse's digestive system is still fundamentally the same as that of his ancestors. The front teeth and lips select and pick up food while the rear teeth grind it, and this chewing and grinding action begins the digestive process.

Horses chew very thoroughly with repeated sweeps of the jaws. Because the top jaw is wider than the bottom one, the chewing action can create sharp edges and hooks on the lower back teeth and upper front teeth, which may injure the mouth. Many problem behaviours in horses can be traced back to a failure to accept the bit because of a sore mouth. Every horse should have his teeth checked by a vet or equine dental technician at least once a year, and more often for young or old animals (see pages 188–189).

The stomach

As the horse swallows, the food enters the gullet from where it passes to the stomach. The horse's stomach is relatively small, holding only about 2.5 kg (5½ lb) of feed maximum at any time. It works best when two-thirds full and should not be over-filled – hence the rule of feeding a horse little and often (see pages 66–67). In the stomach, food is pummelled by the muscular walls, while acid digestive juices, enzymes and a few microbes start to break it down.

The small intestine

From here food passes into the small intestine, which is where the concentrated part of the feed (grain and cubes or nuts) is digested, and the nutrients are absorbed through its walls. The small intestine is a narrow tube about 21 m (70 ft) long where sugars, starches, proteins and oils, plus some minerals and vitamins, are broken down and pass into the bloodstream via the capillary network.

The large intestine

The largest part of the horse's digestive tract is the large intestine. It is here, in a part called the caecum, that the vital fibre portion of the diet (grass, hay and haylage) is broken down, and this provides the horse with most of his energy.

The horse cannot break down fibre by himself – he has evolved a system by which he allows bacteria and other microbes living in the hindgut (large intestine) to do so by fermenting the fibre. The product of this process is an excellent and natural source of energy for the horse, called volatile fatty acids. The microbial population will adapt to match the diet, so any sudden changes to a horse's food will

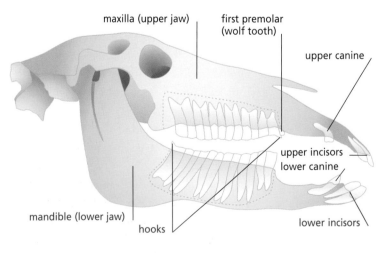

maxilla (upper jaw)

first premolar
(wolf tooth)

upper canine

upper incisors
lower canine

mandible (lower jaw)

hooks

lower incisors

DO

• Feed only clean, good quality feed. Bad food can cause colic (abdominal pain).
• Regard fibre (hay, haylage, grass) as the most important part of the diet.
• Feed cereals only if really necessary.
• Keep the diet as consistent as possible, making any changes very slowly (over several weeks).

DON'T

• Feed your horse erratically, changing ingredients between feeds 'for a change'.
• Limit your horse's fibre ration unless he is eating too much or on veterinary advice.
• Fall for advertising hype. Check with a veterinary surgeon or equine nutritionist before buying supplements, additives or feeds that claim they will turn your horse into a world-beater.
• Use dirty utensils or containers as these can breed bacteria, put your horse off his feed and may possibly cause intestinal infections, which could be serious.

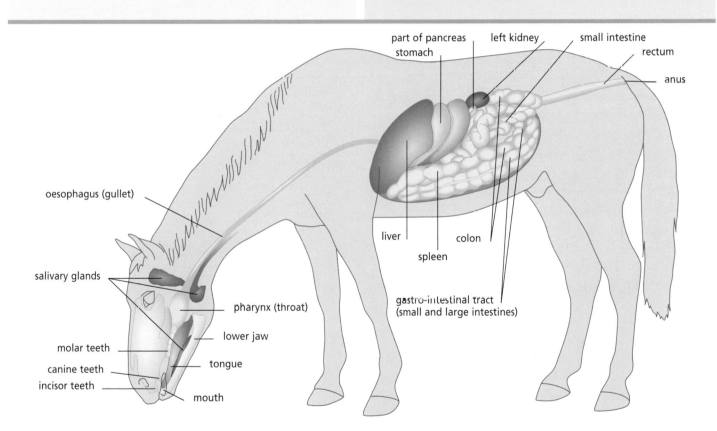

cause upsets because the wrong microbes will be present.

The fermentation that takes place in the caecum is comparable to the rumination of cattle and sheep, but in these animals the process takes place earlier in the system and is much more efficient than in the horse.

Horses that experience digestive problems may benefit from probiotics or prebiotics, which provide beneficial microbes and the nutrients on which they live.

Poor diet

The digestive system is sensitive and digestive disorders in domestic horses fed inappropriately (with too much concentrated food, insufficient fibre, and erratic, widely spaced feeding times) are very common. The blockages that sometimes occur at the pelvic flexure are usually caused by feeding the horse too much indigestible fibre such as poor hay, coarse, dry grass or straw – particularly a lot of wheat straw.

The urinary system

The horse's body is roughly 70 per cent water, and the fluid balance within it is vital to his health. It seems easy to give a horse a bucket of water and expect him to drink normally – but remember the old saying 'you can take a horse to water but you can't make him drink'. Water is more necessary to life than food, yet most owners barely think about it despite spending a lot of time refining their horse's diet.

Checklist
- ✓ the kidneys are a filter
- ✓ they regulate fluid balance
- ✓ effects of toxins and waste products
- ✓ how the kidneys work
- ✓ the process of urination

The kidneys

The kidneys filter the blood and lymph passing through them to remove waste products, toxins, nitrogenous waste (urea) formed by the liver when processing protein, and small particles of tissue debris for passing out in the urine. Some useful substances are reabsorbed for use by the body. The kidneys also excrete excess water in the body and retain water to some extent when the horse is short of it, so helping to regulate the vital fluid balance. The body's chemical balance is also maintained by the kidneys.

This role of regulating the fluid balance is easier when the horse is drinking normally or copiously. When he is not drinking enough, due to either exhaustion or sickness, the job becomes harder and the urine that is excreted will contain a higher level of waste products and be thicker.

How the kidneys work

As in other mammals, the horse has two kidneys placed in the loin area just behind where the saddle would sit, protected by thick layers of fat and by muscle. Each has a tube, the ureter, running from it to the bladder. From here, another tube, the urethra, runs to the vagina or penis.

The familiar indentation in the kidney's shape (hilus) is where blood, lymph and nerves enter. The ureter also leaves the kidney at this point, carrying away urine. There is a collecting area or reservoir (renal pelvis) in the kidney surrounded by the 'medulla', which contains collecting tubules (nephrons). These extend to the outer part of the kidney (cortex), which contains filtering capsules served by capillaries. This is where the vital job of 'cleansing' the blood takes place and useful substances are reabsorbed for recycling.

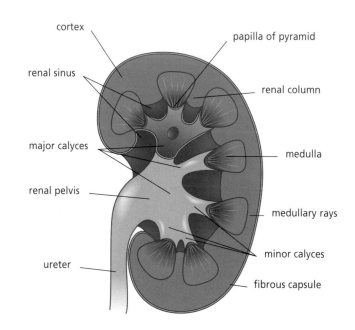

cortex
papilla of pyramid
renal sinus
renal column
major calyces
medulla
renal pelvis
medullary rays
minor calyces
ureter
fibrous capsule

Kidney care

- Keep an eye on your horse's urine and his staling habits.
- Urine can be clear or cloudy and pale yellow in colour.
- If your horse tries to stale frequently with little or no success, he could have an infection and needs veterinary attention.
- Some kidney problems produce symptoms similar to colic (see pages 184–185).

The waste products and excess water empty into the renal pelvis and pass down each kidney's ureter to the bladder, where they are stored as urine. As the bladder fills, pressure on sensory nerve endings causes messages to pass to the central nervous system in the spinal cord. Messages are then sent down motor nerves, instructing the muscles in the bladder wall to squeeze and empty it.

Kidney problems

In the disorder azoturia, in which muscle tissue is damaged and the muscle pigment myoglobin is released, there is a danger of kidney damage due to larger particles of tissue than can pass through the filtering system being released into the blood and passing to the kidneys. In this disease, the urine is the colour of red wine.

Excessive amounts of toxins and waste products in the bloodstream can also cause kidney damage, as can certain diseases. If exhausted dehydrated horses are not treated, again kidney damage may occur.

Encourage your horse to drink by ensuring his water is clean (not topped up instead of changed or contaminated by even tiny amounts of food, bedding or droppings) and in a clean container. Some horses will refuse to drink out of plastic or rubber containers.

Did you know...?

The horse will normally stale (urinate) about four to six times a day and pass about 10 litres (18 pints) of urine in 24 hours. This amount can soon soak the bedding in an average-sized stable – so it probably seems a lot more.

Urination

The horse has a good deal of control over when and where he will urinate, but it is very bad management to force a horse to hold his urine to the point of discomfort and distress. This can easily happen when travelling, because most horses will not stale when the vehicle is in motion, so frequent stops (at least every two hours) should be made on lengthy journeys and, if necessary, the horse unloaded on to a soft surface.

Horses hate splashing themselves with urine and much prefer to stale on an absorbent surface such as earth, grass or bedding. The modern fashion for keeping horses with no bedding in the stable, just rubber or synthetic matting, either during the day or all the time, could be said to be poor management because the horse will delay staling until he is forced to go.

Watch your horse's staling (urination) habits carefully. Any difficulty in straddling the hind legs could indicate injury or a back problem, which can discourage the horse from staling freely.

Mating and foaling

The horse's sexual instincts are highly developed but are often drastically interfered with in domestication. Feral horses, and domestic ones allowed to breed naturally or almost so, have higher conception rates than those mated in hand (held by handlers), with the mare restrained and the pair not allowed to 'court'. Many experts now recommend more natural mating on both economic and ethical grounds.

Checklist
✔ the fertile stallion
✔ the mare's breeding cycle
✔ mating in the wild
✔ mating in domestication
✔ the foaling process
✔ unwanted sexual behaviours

The stallion

Stallions normally reach maximum reproductive capacity by four years old, after which there is usually no change in the daily sperm production by the testicles until they are around 20 years old.

The penis lies within the prepuce (sheath). Debris from the glands and skin lining the sheath accumulates and forms a thick, greasy substance called smegma within the sheath and on the penis. The penis and sheath should be washed about once every two weeks, with warm water, to remove the smegma. This also applies to geldings. Rinse the area thoroughly afterwards.

Rigs

A cryptorchid – a male horse with one or two undescended testicles – is known as a 'rig'. Rigs behave like stallions because their hormone production is the same and they can be fertile. They should be castrated, because the testicles in the abdominal cavity will be at a higher temperature than those in the cooler scrotum and this can induce testicular tumours.

If hormones are still circulating, rigs can be difficult to handle and are sometimes dangerous. A blood test will check the hormone levels and show whether a horse has been castrated successfully or whether he is, in fact, a rig.

Stallions often lead very lonely, artificial lives in domesticity. Living alone is frightening to a feral horse, and frustrating and distressing to a domesticated one.

The mare

Most mares reach sexual maturity at two years old, but they can reach maturity earlier. (It is not recommended that young mares are used for breeding because they often do not have a regular cycle until they are three years old, which makes it very difficult to get them in foal. In addition, the drain of pregnancy on the system of a growing filly can stunt her and the resulting foal may be small and weak.)

A normal mare's cycle will occur in late spring, summer and autumn because it is stimulated by the number of hours of daylight. Some mares do, however, continue to cycle throughout the winter. Gestation lasts for roughly 11 months, so most mares will foal in spring and early summer.

The average oestrus cycle lasts for 21 days but it is variable, often being longer in spring and shorter in summer. The follicular phase, or oestrus (when an egg ripens), when the mare is 'in season', lasts for about six days. The mare is receptive to the stallion throughout oestrus: the vulva appears relaxed, the tail is frequently lifted and the clitoris is everted ('winking').

Mating

Feral equines and those running free in domesticity take mating for granted and youngsters learn by watching, making the mating process less stressful for young breeding stock.

The wise stallion will court a mare for a day or two. When he thinks she is ready, he will approach her from the side to enquire if he may mate her, to avoid being kicked. If she is ready, she will stand for him, he will mount and they will copulate. This may continue for a day or two until the mare goes out of season.

On domestic studs, often the mare is hobbled (her legs tied), twitched (with a rope loop twisted around her upper lip, to cause the release of natural calming substances) and held throughout the process. The stallion is brought in and, held throughout, mounts and serves the mare. The two are then separated and may not meet again.

Foaling

Mares prefer to foal at night, either in a small paddock, their normal grazing field or a large loose box bedded down with clean straw (not shavings, as these get everywhere and stick to everything).

To some extent, mares can delay the act of foaling until they are alone. If watched and the attendant leaves for a short while, the foal will often be there when they return. The foal is born in a membranous sac (amnion), usually forefeet first. The sac usually breaks naturally and the foal starts to breathe. It is good practice to allow mare and foal to lie and rest while (many believe) blood continues to pump down the umbilical cord to the foal. After some minutes this will cease and the cord should break naturally when the mare stands. The whole birthing process may take just a few minutes or an hour or more.

Natural mating normally results in higher conception rates than in horses and ponies that are artificially mated (restrained in hand).

After ensuring that the newborn foal and his dam are healthy and normal, it is usually best to leave them mainly alone for 24 hours to enable them to learn to recognize each other.

Behaviour in the wild

A herd's preoccupations are survival and reproduction so that the species continues. Wild behaviour comprises mainly eating – a major part of survival. Reproduction ensures the continuation of the herd to enable the safety of numbers. The horse's main defence against danger is to gallop away. These factors class horses as grazing, social, running prey animals – behaviour that has ensured their survival for millions of years.

Checklist

✓ structure of the herd
✓ bachelor bands
✓ stallion supremacy
✓ the hierarchy controversy
✓ how horses communicate
✓ body language
✓ the herd's year

Horses feel safer with plenty of space. These feral horses have the protection of each other and space to run away if danger threatens.

Did you know...?

Wild stallions do not grab and keep as many mares as they can. Frequently, when a strange mare tries to join the herd it is the stallion that shoos her away, not the other mares. This seems to be because the stallion understands how many horses a particular area of grazing can support, and also how many mares he can serve and retain.

Herd composition

A feral herd may consist of two or three mares with their 'followers' (offspring of various ages). There will usually be a stallion, although the herd can survive without him on a day-to-day basis, his main purpose being to impregnate the mares once a year. He may hold his position for a few years before a younger or stronger stallion comes along and ousts him.

The sexually mature youngsters, particularly the colts (males), are often kicked out of the herd by the stallion. Sometimes fillies (young females) also have to leave, although stallions are more tolerant of them. Most stallions, though, will not mate with their daughters. Sometimes fillies are 'kidnapped' by other stallions looking to form herds of their own, and sometimes they leave voluntarily to join a stallion.

Bachelor bands are formed by newly pubertal colts for safety, or by older, ousted stallions, and they get on very well until mares come on the scene. Stallions fighting and screaming are terrifying to witness and battles can take hours to settle, sometimes resulting in serious injury to or death of the loser.

Is there a herd hierarchy?

This is proving a vexed question, even among scientists and professional 'observers' of equines in the wild. Even very experienced and well-qualified experts may fail to agree. Most experienced horse people, scientists or not, feel that there is a hierarchy of sorts, although maybe no single leader. It is generally agreed that the stallion is not the leader but an older mare, and even here the word 'leader' may not be accurate.

A wise, experienced mare will know all the best grazing, sheltering, drinking and resting spots, and others will follow her instinctively when she selects where to go. Because acceptance by a herd is vital to equine survival, horses need to be reassured of their place, and will test out other members to see how secure their slot is. Again, this is something experts disagree about but most are of the opinion that it does happen.

Death in the herd

When a new stallion takes over a herd, it is common for him to kill young foals sired by the previous stallion. Cruel and counter-productive though this may sound, it may be done so that the new stallion can remove his predecessor's genes and concentrate on promoting his own bloodline. He is less likely to try to kill older youngsters because they can put up a good fight in return, but he will probably kick the males out of his new herd.

Communication

Horses communicate mainly by means of 'body language', although there is some vocalization in the form of whinnying, neighing, snorting and soft whickering. Their communication signals and postures are instinctive, as are their vocal sounds, and horses the world over understand each other. It is clear that they do not have a learned language in the way we do.

Nostril to nostril, these horses are communicating, maybe an invitation for mutual grooming or a warning to keep away from each other's foals.

The herd's year

Spring Breeding, feeding up after winter, formation of new herds in response to circulation of 'breeding hormones'. Natural weaning of last year's foal, if new foal expected.

Summer Breeding, foaling, eating, relaxation; avoiding excessively hot sun, weather and insects.

Autumn Winding down for winter, mares' seasons shorter and not so fertile, foals more independent of dams but still together. 'Autumn flush' of carbohydrate in grass helps to build up body weight for the coming winter.

Winter In 'survival' mode, looking for sheltered areas to conserve body heat, condition and energy. Foraging for whatever food is available. No interest in breeding, mares not in season. Youngsters now taking very little milk.

Horses move others out of their personal space and protect their foals by:
• putting their ears back
• wrinkling their nostrils up and back
• putting the head and neck down
• swishing the tail.

To another horse this clearly means 'go away'. If the second horse is weaker or more insecure than the first, he will move away, but if he feels like trying his luck he may stand up to the first with similar gestures and there may be a scuffle, with biting, kicking and striking out.

Acceptance and welcome are signalled by:
• ears pricked
• eyes soft
• nostrils relaxed
• tail softly relaxed, too.
A soft whickering noise may be made.

Alarm and fear are shown by:
• head up
• ears pricked strongly towards the danger
• wide and wild eyes
• tail up and a prancing gait
• possibly a canter or gallop away from the danger.

Behaviour in domestication

Captive, domestic horses possess all the natural instincts of their feral cousins – they are just not allowed to express most of them. In a domestic paddock, the herd formation will be very artificial. On some livery yards, mares and geldings are separated when grazing. Stabled horses live unnaturally restricted lives but, if not over-confined, may come to associate their stables with shelter, safety, food and water.

Checklist
- ✓ effects of domestic management
- ✓ 'stereotypical' behaviours
- ✓ manage the horse for the animal he is
- ✓ clarity, consistency and timing in training

Stereotypical behaviours

These are the main difference between the behaviour of feral and domesticated horses. They include:

- Crib biting
- Wind sucking
- Box walking
- Weaving
- Head twisting and nodding
- Tongue lolling
- Wood scraping and chewing despite good diet
- Kicking walls and door
- Pawing floor
- Tearing clothing (e.g. rugs)

Stereotypical behaviours used to be known as 'stable vices'. They are repetitive and apparently purposeless behaviours performed by domesticated, usually stabled, horses and are never seen in feral horses. This makes it certain that it is the living conditions we impose on horses that are responsible for these behaviours. There is no question of the horse having a 'vice', as was indicated by the traditional term.

Top tip

By watching how a particular horse behaves with others of his own kind, you can learn a lot about how he responds to different situations.

Being stabled for too long and denied physical contact with his friends, plus insufficient fibre, is a very common cause of unhappiness.

Spring tantrums

All horses, including geldings, will behave like over-enthusiastic youngsters in spring when hormones awake from winter. This annual spring phenomenon is normal, to be expected, and to be coped with using tolerance and a reasonable degree of control and discipline. Horses will be horses, and should be allowed to be.

The performance of stereotypes is much more widespread than previously recognized and can include any natural behaviour performed in an apparently pointless manner, and any behaviour pattern not seen in feral horses.

Just as outdated and counter-productive as calling these actions stable vices is the still widespread practice of physically trying to stop a horse performing them. It is now acknowledged by both scientists and caring horse keepers that stereotypies provide a horse with an outlet for distress – the distress caused by unsuitable living conditions.

Is there a cure?

Once certain stereotypes have become ingrained habits, it is not possible to 'cure' them completely. Even if a horse's management is improved vastly and the behaviour greatly reduced or even apparently cured, should the right conditions recur the horse will resume his 'problem behaviour'. It is believed that the predisposition to performing some of these behaviours is genetically pre-programmed in some horses.

There is no doubt, however, that good management, more close social interaction, ample fibre and water, plenty of space and movement at liberty, and shelter facilities reduce the performance of stereotypes in many horses.

Behaviour towards humans

Horses tend to treat humans and other animals as they would another horse. They use the same body language and sounds, which we can learn well enough. What we, understandably, find troublesome is the horse's natural tendency to defend himself, when he feels it necessary, by biting and kicking, and to avoid what causes him discomfort, pain, fear or distress – usually his work or handling procedures.

To be fair to the horse and establish a mutually acceptable working relationship, it is essential that horse owners, keepers, trainers and riders learn to manage and work horses appropriately for the type of animal they are. Clear, consistent requests by voice and physical aids are vital if the horse is to associate them with what is wanted and form the habit of complying. Also essential is instant reward and correction so that, again, the horse understands what is wanted and what is not. He will learn this by association if your timing is truly instant. He will soon learn the approving tone in which you say 'good boy' and, likewise, the slightly sterner tone of 'no'.

These horses can see each other but this is not enough. Friends should be stabled next to each other and be able to touch and sniff each other, preferably over their partitions, or at least through 'chat holes'.

YOUR FIRST HORSE

It is often not long before someone who starts riding at a riding school or on friends' horses begins to realize how restricting it is not having a horse of their own and decides to buy one. Other people have ridden for years but have never had their own horse because of circumstances – work, money, practicalities, problems finding good livery and so on. It is not a decision to be taken lightly, and although you may find that ownership does away with one set of problems, it introduces another – involving expense, time, relationship with your horse and responsibility.

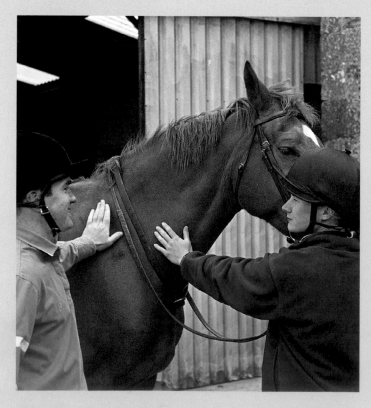

Are you ready to own a horse?

Buying and owning a horse is not always straightforward, but if you plan carefully and have the time and money available, horse ownership is one of the most rewarding enterprises in which you could be involved. Horses are fascinating animals, but new owners are often taken aback at how much time they take up and how expensive they are to maintain.

Checklist

✓ how well do you ride?
✓ do you have time to look after a horse?
✓ can you afford it?
✓ choose your horse realistically
✓ suitable livery options

How good a rider are you?

This is the first thing you should consider: nothing puts you off quicker than a horse you are wary or even frightened of riding. Riding is a potentially dangerous sport, but following sensible safety guidelines reduces the risks. One of these guidelines is to buy a horse on which you feel comfortable and safe, that is well behaved, and which you can cope with both on the ground and in the saddle.

How much time do you have?

Time and money are inextricably linked where horses are concerned. If you want to save time and have no family or anyone else available who will help you with the many chores for nothing, you will have to pay to have your horse looked after. Whether you 'do' your horse yourself or not, you need to be aware of the time involved. You should reckon on at least two hours a day every day of the year, and this probably won't include travelling to and from the yard, and riding itself.

Owning a horse on whom you feel safe and happy and who seems to like you, too, is worth more than words can say.

Top tip

One of the best ways to find out how good you are is to attend a good riding school and have a course of lessons aimed at testing you and improving your riding, too. Then ask the teacher how good they think you are and what sort of horse, cob or pony would be suitable for you. It would also be a good plan to take a course of horse-care lessons, because this is an aspect of horse ownership that catches out most first-time owners.

How much money can you spare?

However much your livery yard owner quotes you for, say, part livery, you can certainly double it. It is amazing how much extra expenditure crops up – continually – for such things as tack and rugs, shoeing, veterinary costs, travelling, extra feed, competition expenses, and your own clothes and equipment. Realistically you cannot keep horses well on a shoestring budget.

Daily horse tasks

- Turning the horse out into the field and bringing him in again at the end of the day.
- Mucking out and bedding down.
- Grooming.
- Tacking up and untacking.
- Rugging up and off-rugging.
- Mixing feeds, washing buckets/manger, taking feed to horse.
- Filling hay tubs or nets.
- Filling water buckets/troughs.

Cleaning your tack is one of many time-consuming but essential 'horse chores'. Most owners, though, regard these chores as part of the fun.

What kind of horse do you want?

Don't be tempted by a glamorous, breedy, highly strung, expensive animal if you don't need him or cannot ride or handle him safely. Whatever you choose, you must feel physically comfortable on him, so he must not be too big or too small (the soles of your feet should be about level with the horse's breastbone when you are mounted). If the horse is too wide or too narrow for your leg length you will be uncomfortable, and if the horse is not well behaved and as safe as a horse reasonably can be, you may lose your nerve rather quickly. Your horse should be a friend with a good temperament, and you must actually like him.

Where are you going to keep him?

For your first horse, it is strongly advised that you keep him at a good riding school or livery stable. Here you will have plenty of professional guidance available from the owner and staff, and they will be able to step in and help you when necessary. Unless your family has a lot of experience in coping with horses, keeping him at home is not a good plan.

Do-it-yourself livery yards are not recommended for first-time horse owners, as you may not have enough experience to look after your horse properly without professional guidance – and well-meant advice from other owners may not be appropriate.

If you love horses, having one of your own, and with whom you get on well, is one of the most fulfilling ways of life.

Keeping a horse at livery

Most owners do not have or cannot afford a home suitable for keeping a horse. Renting accommodation, plus paying for some services, is the usual solution. Keeping a horse at livery is the most common way of accommodating him, but is also the most expensive (other than paying your own groom), depending on the services you need. Livery brings its own problems but, with good grace, these can usually be resolved.

Checklist
- ✓ types of livery
- ✓ services provided
- ✓ choosing a livery yard
- ✓ a place of your own
- ✓ sharing responsibility

Ample periods of liberty are essential to contented horses, so enquire carefully about a livery yard's turn-out services and facilities before you choose.

Full livery

The most expensive kind of livery, the services offered as full livery vary widely according to where you live. It usually means that a stable, grazing (although often not in winter) and hay or haylage are provided, plus some basic services such as feeding and watering, daily quartering (brushing over), picking out feet, changing rugs and mucking out. The yard proprietor should also turn out your horse in some suitable area for exercise, including in winter and, hopefully, grazing. You may well have to buy your own bedding and extra feed, supplements and so on, and will certainly have to pay your own veterinary and farriery expenses.

Part livery

A stable and turnout should be provided, as well as hay or haylage and morning and/or evening feeding (though you will have to pay for the feed itself) and watering. The staff may also turn out and bring in your horse and skip out the stable (pick up droppings), depending on what you have agreed.

Do-it-yourself livery

Your rent should include a stable and turnout/grazing facility, and possibly hay or haylage, but no services or extras of any kind. Owners usually have a system whereby they help each other on difficult days or during sickness or holidays. If this system is not in place on your yard, you will need a high level of commitment *every* day.

Other types of livery

Grass livery Your horse is kept at grass all year round with no stable and often no adequate shelter, either. This is not suitable for most animals at most times of year. Ground conditions can vary widely from baked hard in summer to a quagmire in winter. Insects can cause great misery as can burning hot sun, driving wind, sustained heavy rain and other extremes of weather.

Working livery Your horse is used for clients at the riding centre. This can work for or against him, according to the quality of the riders, and for or against you, depending on when he is available for you to ride.

Schooling livery Your horse will be schooled or trained, usually over a limited period of weeks, but not used for clients. This is expensive unless you negotiate to look after your horse yourself during his stay.

This stable door is clearly too high for this poor little pony. Make sure your horse's stable is big enough for him and that he can see out comfortably.

The inside of this box is very dark, indicating that there is no other look-out point or even a window that will admit some light and more fresh air.

Assessing a livery stable

By far the most important thing to look at closely is the condition and demeanour of the horses. If there is a high percentage of horses performing stereotypical behaviours (see pages 42–43) or looking unhappy or restless in their stables, be suspicious. If there appears to be ample turnout but all the horses are indoors, be suspicious.

In general, the horses should appear content, pleasant, comfortable, and both cared for and cared about, otherwise yours may be at risk and you will also be unhappy tolerating a bad atmosphere.

A little peeling paintwork, bedding not swept up and minor untidiness is not important. What should put you right off are miserable horses, surly, unprofessional staff, dirty beds, mangers and rugs, horses left without hay and water, a muck heap very close to stables and similar features. You need reasonable cleanliness and hygiene, and a proprietor and staff you can talk to and trust.

Renting or buying land and stables

There is a way around livery problems and that is to rent not simply a stable and grazing on someone else's yard but a whole yard yourself, or even just a field with a shelter. If you have spare accommodation, you could rent out stables and grazing to other owners, or give them free use in exchange for help with your horse. This would reduce the restrictions on your time, *if* you can find knowledgeable and trustworthy people.

If you can manage to buy your own land and stables, this may not only give you more peace of mind (provided your security arrangements are excellent) but also prove to be a good investment. Such properties are much cheaper than buying a house with land – most owners' dream – which is out of the reach of most horse and pony owners.

Questions to ask at a livery yard

- What exactly do I get for my money?
- Who will be looking after my horse?
- What are the turnout and grazing arrangements, year round?
- Are there any restrictions on using the schooling facilities?
- What does your insurance cover?
- Do you provide a livery contract?
- What precautions can be taken to introduce my horse safely to others?
- If he is unhappy in his stable, can I move him to another?
- What are your security arrangements?
- May I use my own vet, farrier, trainer and other specialists for my horse?

Keeping your horse at home

Most experienced owners dream of having their horse outside their back door. Provided your facilities are reasonable, this gives you complete freedom over how you look after him, when he can be turned out, when you can ride and umpteen other matters. However, it is a big commitment and if you are not experienced and knowledgeable, you can inadvertently put your own and your horse's lives in danger.

Checklist
✓ permissions and legalities
✓ land and stables
✓ other horses
✓ managing your yard
✓ getting help
✓ consider your neighbours
✓ where to ride

Permission

Different regions of different countries have varying requirements for accommodating large animals such as horses. You can ask local horse owners who keep horses at home if they have had problems with this, to help you prepare your case when you contact your local council.

Facilities

Most horses of any type do well living outside with adequate shelter. Contrary to popular opinion, you can get them very fit living like this, and they are usually more content and healthier. You will need at least 1 hectare (2.4 acres) of well-drained, productive land for one horse, and half that again for each additional horse, if you want to make grass a significant part of their diet. You will need to be able to divide up the land so that each part can be alternately grazed, treated and rested.

A strong, roomy, man-made shelter of some kind should be provided, and a stable is useful for occasional confinement such as veterinary treatment or to bring horses in at night in winter and during the day in summer. You will also need storage for feed, bedding and tack.

Company

Horses that are happy living alone are very rare. Most need another horse or pony for company, but pairs often become inseparable. This is something to think about carefully. If you have the space, it is often a good plan to have three or more horses in total, some of them belonging to friends who can help out with the responsibilities.

Help

You need to decide whether members of your family will be able to help with the horses when you are at work, sick or away. You also need to work out what to do with the horses during family holidays. They could be sent away on temporary livery, or a live-in freelance or agency groom might come to stay.

To keep a horse at home you need high levels of commitment, reliable help and basic facilities. Your horse will also certainly need company.

Access

It is wise (and may be a legal requirement) to have access for a large vehicle such as a fire engine or for feed deliveries – or, should it come to it, to remove the carcass of a dead horse.

Neighbours

To avoid possible unpleasantness for neighbours, you will need to make every effort to minimize smells from your muck heap and possible inconvenience caused by vehicles delivering feed and bedding to your premises. You can muck out straight into plastic sacks and ask delivery drivers to switch off their engines when parked to cut down pollution and noise, and to park considerately if your neighbour's access is affected.

Riding out

You may be lucky enough to have an outdoor arena at home but, even so, few horses stay sane and content just being ridden round and round in a confined space. Do you live in an area with good hacking, or do you have your own transport (and space to park it) so that you can travel your horse to nearby safe hacking areas?

If keeping your horse at home, consider where you are going to ride. Most horses soon become bored working only in an arena. Good hacking facilities are advised.

Managing muck

Disposing of dirty bedding and droppings can be a major headache. Ask local owners what they do.

• Consider bagging droppings into strong plastic sacks for local gardeners to take away, returning the sacks.

• Dirty bedding may need to be bagged and taken to the local tip.

• Your council may remove your muck heap.

• Alternatively, offer it to local plant nurseries.

• If you have a muck heap, it should be sited downwind of the stables and any nearby housing, for health reasons.

DO

• Keep on top of regular chores such as muck removal before they become a problem.

• Provide reasonably hard standing in at least one area, maybe outside a barn or stables, so that your horses do not need to be shut in when your land is too wet to turn them out.

• Make sure your horses have ready access to clean water that is relatively easy for you to provide.

• Check with your insurance company about including your horse and related equipment in your household policy.

DON'T

• Advertise the fact that you have horses at home. Equestrian equipment is very attractive to thieves.

• Have your paddock gates opening on to a public road or right of way, if you can avoid it.

• Let your place become messy and smelly, both for your own sake and to minimize complaints from neighbours.

• Make a lot of noise in the stable yard late at night if you have neighbours close by. Clattering buckets, radios playing and bright lights are asking for trouble.

Where to find your horse

It is not until you decide to buy a horse that you discover how difficult it can be to find one that is what you want and is suitable. Lots of time, money, frustration and disappointment can be involved in your search. Sadly, many sellers are not honest and a first-time buyer should always take along a very experienced friend or professional who can ask the right questions and assess horses astutely.

Checklist
- ✓ reputable dealers
- ✓ exchanging an unsuitable horse
- ✓ private buys can be risky
- ✓ use a professional equine consultant
- ✓ riding school horses
- ✓ buying a specific breed
- ✓ a horse on loan

Dealers

The advantage of buying from a dealer is that, firstly, it is not in their interests to lie about the qualities of the horse they sell you and, secondly, if things don't work out between you and your horse you can take it back to the dealer to exchange, or part exchange, for another. The dealer obviously has to make a profit and you may lose some money on such a transaction, but it is usually worth it in the end. Good dealers are discovered through word of mouth and advertisements in the equestrian or farming press.

Advertisements

Buying a horse from a private seller through an advertisement can be quite risky. As already advised, you should take an experienced person with you when viewing horses. You could approach a professional teacher or equestrian consultant, or perhaps a qualified member of staff from your riding school.

Don't make the mistake of falling for the first head that appears over a door. Be prepared to take time and trouble over your choice.

Riding schools

Buying your favourite mount from your riding school might sound like a good idea, but horses can change dramatically away from a familiar environment. This particularly applies to horses that are used to working for several hours a day. Such horses often become almost unmanageable on the much lighter work regime of a private home, even on a low-energy diet. However, it is worth giving it a try, but make sure you have a similar arrangement as with a dealer and can return the horse if something goes wrong.

Friends and contacts

Friends and acquaintances who have horses themselves will often know of animals that are available but are not on the open market. After this, proceed as if buying through an advertisement, and take a consultant with you when viewing horses.

Charities

Many charities are keen to rehome their rescued and rehabilitated horses. You can get a horse on permanent loan from them and, provided you treat him well, he will be with you for the rest of his life. The charity will carry out a home check (including quizzing you about your knowledge and seeing you ride). Once you have the horse at home, you are normally responsible for all his expenses. Many people and horses become happily matched in this way.

Breed societies

If you want a horse of a specific breed, or a cross of that breed, you can approach breed societies, who usually run sales lists. Many will be youngsters for sale by their breeders but, as a first-timer, you are advised to buy an older, trained horse – there are usually a few on the list. If you do want a specific breed or type, you may need to travel quite a distance to try out a suitable horse, but if he fulfils your dream it will be worth it.

Surf the net

The internet is now a well-established way to find horses for sale, so key in what you want, click 'search' and sit back.

Loaning

Loaning, or borrowing, a horse from another private owner is a possibility, particularly if there is an option to buy should you and the horse really suit each other. For the sake

of the three of you, however, you should make out a detailed loan agreement stipulating precisely what the conditions are and get it checked by a solicitor to ensure it is legally enforceable.

Frequently asked question

Q A couple of years ago I loaned a horse from an acquaintance who said I could have the horse for the rest of his life – at my own expense, of course. Now she has said she wants him back, despite the fact that he is well cared for and I love him very much. Can she just come and take him? I am really upset.

A If you did not have a written loan agreement drawn up it could be difficult for you to keep the horse. Certainly the owner cannot force her way on to your property. However, if she has paperwork to prove that the horse is her legal property it seems likely that you will have to let him go. Go and see a solicitor to discuss the matter.

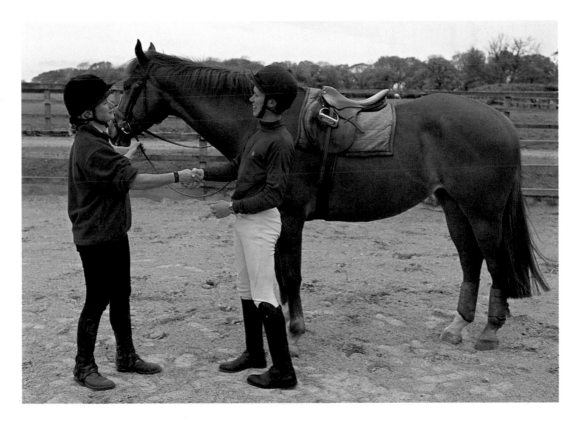

Talk to friends and acquaintances, who may reveal sources for you to investigate. Your riding school may recommend a good dealer – particularly if you are going to keep your horse at livery with them.

The right horse for you

Horses come in all shapes and sizes, not to mention all stages of training and all temperaments. People have created hundreds of different breeds, of which some will be easily available in your country and some will not. It is best to start out with a reasonably clear idea of what you want (but do not over-horse yourself with something you cannot manage). However, stay flexible in your ideas or you may miss a treasure.

Checklist
- ✓ size, shape and strength
- ✓ the importance of temperament
- ✓ breed and type
- ✓ age and experience
- ✓ stage of training

These two riders of obviously different heights have horses suited to each of them – also of different heights.

Size

This is probably the most important factor for an inexperienced rider. If the horse is too big, he can appear somewhat intimidating; too small, and you start to feel that you should not be up there anyway.

Most horses, large or small, are very capable of carrying an average-sized adult. However, you will feel more

Stage of schooling

For a first-time owner, a horse needs to:

• Stand still on command. This is extremely important.

• Move off at the requested gait – walk or trot – and perform his transitions from one gait to another without argument, bucking, pulling, cavorting around or generally frightening his inexperienced rider.

• Jump small obstacles, if requested, without argument – provided the rider asks correctly and reasonably.

• Have a correct way of going (which riding school lessons should have taught you), but to be fair to him you must be capable of maintaining his performance.

• Be safe in all traffic and similar circumstances (with trains, helicopters, microlite aircraft, farm machinery, roadworks and so on), unless it is certain he will never meet these.

• Be co-operative to handle on the ground (such as good stable manners, good to catch, load, shoe, etc.).

comfortable on one that is the right size for you. The horse's make and shape (known as his conformation) also play an important part. Some small, chunkily built and well-muscled horses can be incredibly strong, while others are light-framed and incapable of carrying anyone too heavy. Generally, it is considered that a horse should be able to carry a rider of about one-sixth of his own weight, cobs and ponies more.

It is important to remember that it is not just the weight of the rider that is important – the saddle and other equipment can significantly increase the load.

It is tempting to kiss your pony, like this, but if you breathe into his nostril you may end up with a nip!

Temperament

A suitable temperament is vital and most riding schools take on only horses or ponies that have proved themselves suitable for beginners. They must be steady and reliable, not too quick, yet responsive enough to react when indicated to do so by an inexperienced rider. All in all, these 'schoolmaster' animals are required to be the perfect mount for a less-than-perfect rider.

Age

Various breeds of horse and pony and their cross-breds are suited to the role of first mount, but good training over a period of time usually means that a slightly older animal is a better bet.

It is not usually a good plan to put a complete beginner on a horse younger than six years old, as the horse is unlikely to have had sufficient experience in varied situations or be far enough on in his training to be thoroughly reliable. A horse is usually backed for riding when he is three to four years old, and is not considered fully mature until he reaches the age of six. The young horse then needs a gradual build-up of work in order to become physically strong enough to cope with the demands placed on him.

It is particularly important not to work youngsters too hard and to leave their schooling to sympathetic, experienced riders.

Ponies and cobs

Plenty of adults ride ponies and cobs – it depends on your height and weight whether this is an option for you, so take advice. These are chunkier animals well up to carrying up to, say, one-quarter of their own weight. A substantial cob is capable of carrying quite a heavy man out hunting, a task it would be quite wrong to inflict on, say, a Thoroughbred or Arab of the same height.

Ponies have a rather more independent nature than horses. They tend to be stronger and tougher for their size and full of character. They can be alternately as generous as you could want and extremely stubborn!

Choosing the right breed

Hot-bloods are named for their sensitivity and temperament. The Arab, Thoroughbred and their cross, the Anglo-Arab, are common hot bloods. They love speed and equable weather.

Cold-bloods such as Shires, Percherons, Clydesdales and others are bigger, massively muscled and bred for hauling heavy weights. They are slower and calmer.

Warm-bloods are crosses between the two. Those without too many hot-blood traits can be good for a first-time owner.

Iberian breeds (the Portuguese Lusitano and the Spanish or Andalusian) form the basis of many American breeds. They are genetically warm-bloods and usually proud but biddable.

All breeds, whether horses or ponies, are a mixture of different types that existed before formal breeds were created by people and bred for very specific purposes, such as carriage work or racing.

Colours and markings

Colour preference is probably largely a personal matter. Breed societies usually stipulate what colour their registered animals may be and state which parts of the body, if any, may bear white hairs. There are also societies for horses of particular colours, such as palominos (golden with white or silver manes and tails) or spotted horses. Colours and markings help to identify a horse or pony when recorded on his documents. Colour may change somewhat with age, the season and exposure to the weather, but markings do not.

Checklist
✓ evolution of colour
✓ solid and broken colours
✓ breed colours
✓ face and leg markings
✓ how pigment works

Origins of colour

All animals develop colour and patterns to help protect them in their evolutionary environments and sometimes to attract mates. In horses, the basis for colours was originally entirely for camouflage – dappling and striping were probably common among primitive types as they protected the animal in forest light patterns. Zebras today may seem to be calling attention to themselves, but in practice a milling herd of striped bodies confuses the eye of a predator, making it difficult to pick out one individual.

Solid colours

More solid colours developed very gradually due to genetic changes. Eventually, those animals of a more solid colour survived better on the new, grassy plains. Ancient colours seem to be the unremarkable dun, bay and maybe roan, plus spots, splashes and dapples. In today's horses, colour is often bred for by humans.

Broken colours

Horses with large, irregular patches of colour and white, such as piebalds, skewbalds, paints and pintos, are showing ancient camouflage patterns. A piebald is black and white and a skewbald is any other colour or colours and white. Paint horses are known as 'coloured' in countries other than the United States.

This horse is a typical palomino in colour – a golden coat and white mane and forelock (and tail). The palomino is registered as a colour and not a breed.

What is melanin ?

Colour is genetically controlled and is produced by a colouring pigment in the skin called melanin. The more melanin that is present, the darker the colour. Melanin is believed to have a protective effect on skin, which does seem to work in practice. True albino horses, with no colouring matter at all in their bodies, have pink skin all over and even pink eyes, which comes from the blood circulating in the eye, normally disguised by colour.

Other markings

Ermine marks Black, brown or chestnut spots on white hairs around the pastern or coronet band.

Zebra markings Black stripes, usually horizontal, on the backs of the forearms or fronts of the second thigh (gaskin), usually found on duns but also on some other colours as well.

Black points Black lower legs, sometimes also taken to include mane, forelock and tail; found on duns, bays and browns.

Breed colours

Certain colours or markings can indicate the age of a specific breed. The dun/buckskin, a golden to golden-brown colour with a black mane and tail and often a dark stripe or line down the spine, is one of these, and several ancient breeds, such as the Norwegian Fjord, have this as a strong basic colour.

Others have distinctive colour characteristics, including the Exmoor pony, with 'mealy' (oatmeal-coloured) hair around the eyes and on the muzzle, the Appaloosa, with striking spots and white membrane around the rims of the eyes, and the Norwegian Fjord, with a distinctive black centre line along the white mane that continues down the back and tail.

Leg markings are named according to the amount of white and, usually, the area.

Face markings

These are described by their shape on the horse's head and include star, stripe, blaze and snip. They are white hair patterns over pink skin, which lacks pigment. Those on the muzzle and around the nostrils are particularly prone (in some individuals) to an allergic reaction to high-nitrogen fertilizer on the land. Pink-skinned areas in general (not only on the face) are often prone to sunburn, too.

Leg markings

These are named according to the amount of white on the leg, such as sock or stocking, and often include the name of the area covered, such as heel or pastern. A complete white area generally corresponds with a white hoof on that leg. An Appaloosa may have striped hooves as well.

Heel or coronet   **Pastern**   **Sock**   **Stocking**   **White leg**

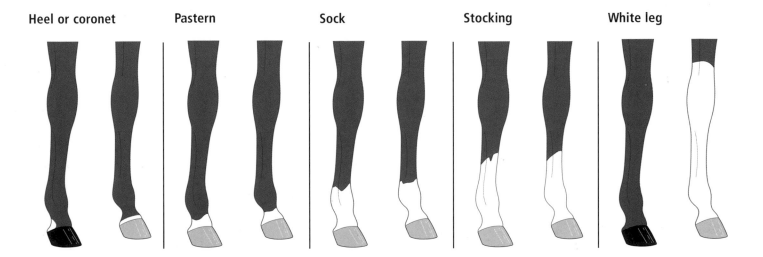

Trying out a horse

You will need to be on your guard during this process, as many sellers do not tell the truth about their horse. They will often have lunged or ridden him before you arrive, have him already stabled and clean, and present a list of plausible-sounding reasons as to why certain tests cannot be applied. Even with today's consumer laws, it is always a case of 'buyer beware'. Do *not* fall in love with the horse at this point.

Checklist

✔ keep your appointment
✔ arrive early
✔ riding the horse
✔ are you interested?
✔ vetting
✔ warranties and trials

Make an appointment

You will need to ring up to make an appointment to try out your potential new horse. If you find that you cannot keep to the arrangement, do ring and cancel or rearrange to save the owner's time and trouble.

Arrival time

It is usually best to arrive up to half an hour early – earlier than this looks suspicious. The reason you should arrive early is to see if anything is being done to the horse that the owner may not want you to see, such as his not wanting to be caught, groomed, have his feet picked out, be tacked up and so on. Sometimes, though, the 'warming-up' will have been done long before your arrival.

Let the owner ride first

You need to see the horse ridden first by a familiar rider in familiar surroundings. If he behaves badly here he will probably be worse with you, unless you feel that he is being ridden or treated badly. For your first horse, you don't want problems. If the horse is anything but pleasant and well behaved now, go no further.

Be aware that a horse may be given a dose of mild tranquillizer before your arrival. An experienced consultant may be able to spot this by the horse's demeanour. Be aware, also, that horses being sold by a professional on behalf of the owner may be 'problem' horses in disguise. If the owner or an 'ordinary' rider cannot show the horse, he could be a difficult one. Horses may also behave well under the eye of their trainer but change when the trainer disappears.

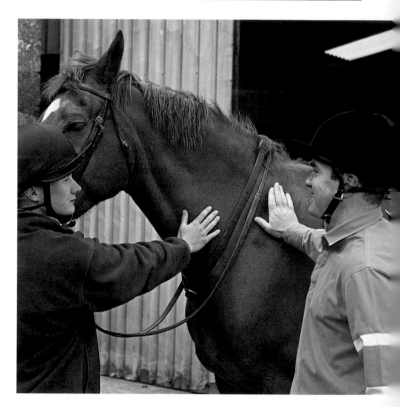

Try to stay emotionally detached and let yourself be guided by the professional consultant you have, hopefully, brought with you.

Let your consultant ride next

The second person to put the horse through his paces should be your consultant and it is as well to be guided by them as to whether or not you should ride him yourself, if you are a novice. An expert can quite quickly get a good feel for whether or not the horse is what you need.

Try the horse yourself

Now it's your turn. You should be able to mount, walk, trot, canter, maybe gallop and jump, dismount and lead the horse in hand with no problems at all. If he needs to be traffic proof, you should watch the owner ride him in traffic before you try him. You should be given an opportunity to handle him on the ground, maybe tack up and untack, rug up and off-rug, handle his feet and so on.

Express interest – or otherwise

If you really like the horse, say that you will have him subject to him passing a veterinary examination. If you really don't want him, say so to save everybody's time.

Make your decision

When you have the results of the veterinary examination, you will be able to make your decision. If you do not understand any part of the report, discuss it carefully with the vet. They may, indeed, advise you not to buy the horse for the purpose you have in mind and, as a first-time buyer, you would be well advised to abide by this advice.

Warranties and trials

A warranty is a guarantee that the horse is as described, but in view of the compensation culture presently pervading most of the western world, they are difficult to get. Wording can be very cunning: often, the owner will state in the warranty that, for instance, the horse has never been known in the past to buck (or whatever). This clearly leaves room for the horse to do so in the future (in your ownership), in which case the previous owner could say that it is your fault the horse has started bucking. You need to discuss this whole topic with a solicitor experienced in horses. Sometimes horses are sold 'on trial', so that you can see whether or not you get on and the horse is all you hoped he would be. You will be responsible for insuring him during this period, from the moment he leaves his present owner. Make sure that, should you return him, you will get all your money back. If you return him in a worse state than when he arrived, you could face legal action from the owner. Again, a solicitor should be able to advise you on this.

Veterinary examinations

Different countries have different requirements from a veterinary examination of a potential purchase. Currently in the UK there are two levels of examination, the higher level (known as the Five Stage vetting) being very stringent. Much depends on what you want the horse to do and how sound he needs to be. The owner's vet cannot be used for this purpose as there will be a conflict of interest, but it saves you travelling charges if you choose a vet from near the horse's home. Discuss first with the vet exactly what you want the horse for and try to be present on the day. Note that some veterinary practices will not now examine horses for purchase in some countries in view of the potential for litigation.

Do not try the horse till the owner and your consultant have ridden him. Be confident, ride well and make your own objective assessment.

GENERAL CARE

No matter what you want to do with a horse, you cannot do it if he is not healthy – and any vet or equine health care professional will tell you that the aspect of horse ownership that best ensures good health is correct care and management appropriate to the particular horse. There are basic elements of care that apply to all horses, but they are also individuals with different likes and dislikes, needs and responses. You would not manage a Shetland gymkhana pony in the same way as a Thoroughbred racehorse. Getting the care right makes your horse feel good – and you, too.

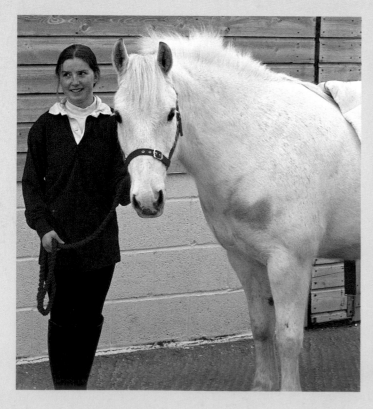

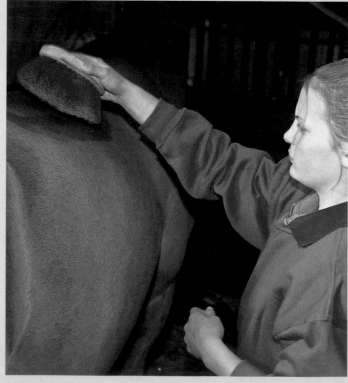

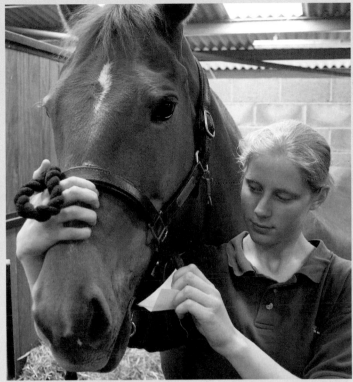

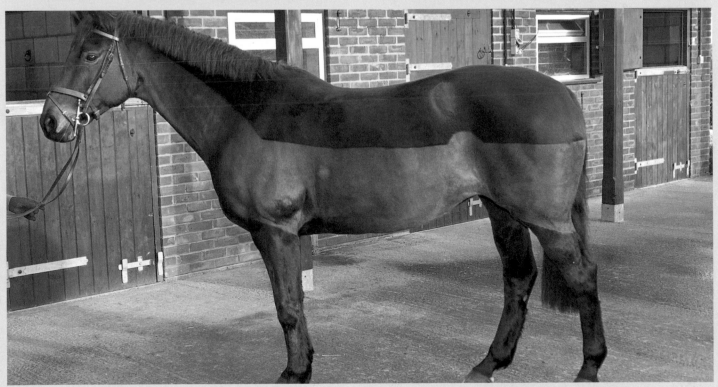

Stables and paddocks

Your horse's stable and turnout, whether pasture or not, are his immediate environment and have a significant effect on his psychological and physical well-being. An ideal arrangement is for a horse to be able to come and go from his stable more or less at will. Even being able to potter about in a smallish space leading off the stable is better than being fully confined, and gives some space and freedom.

Checklist
✓ stables to suit horses
✓ stable size and features
✓ how much grazing?
✓ safe fencing
✓ other horses
✓ pasture management

Stable design

A horse's stable should be light, airy, and preferably give him a view into the distance and into a companion horse's stable. It should also be as large as possible. The latest research indicates that stables need to be about 5 x 5 m ($16\frac{1}{2}$ x $16\frac{1}{2}$ ft) for a horse to feel comfortable.

The American barn system, with rows of stables inside a large building with a central walkway, makes life easier for the people looking after the horses but may not always be the best for the horses. The barn must be well ventilated with views outside, usually from openings on the back walls of the stables that will be closed in bad weather only. In individual outdoor stables, put an extra rug on your horse rather than close the top door, but do not overload him with clothing.

The other prerequisites in a stable are:
• A constant supply of clean, fresh water, accessible from a low level.
• A more or less constant supply of fibre or roughage such as hay, haylage or short-chopped forage feed, again available from a low level.
• Clean, dry bedding when the horse is inside, whether or not the stable is floored with rubber or synthetic matting, so that he can lie down at will and urinate in comfort.

Paddocks

Each horse will need a minimum of 0.2–0.4 hectare ($\frac{1}{2}$–1 acre) of grazing. A horse living out all the time will need at least twice this amount. The better the quality of the grazing, the smaller the area needed. Horses also need space and do better on large areas of poorish grazing. Over-nutritious grass can cause circulatory and digestive problems in ponies and cobs.

Stable safety

Check your stable for anything on which the horse could hurt himself, such as broken wood or metal, nails in the bedding, electric wiring within reach, missing planks or bricks, equipment left in the stable and so on.

Make sure that all your equipment is kept in safe condition and put back in its place after use. Your insurance policy will certainly require that valuable tack is kept locked away, maybe in the house or a very secure tack or harness room.

Troublesome plants

US			UK		
Bracken fern	Oleander	Wild cherry	Beech	Foxglove	Oak
Castor bean	Prince's plume	Wild onion	Box	Hemlock	Privet
Fiddleneck	Rattleweed	Wild tobacco	Bracken	Holly (berries)	Ragwort
Golden week	Red maple	Woody aster	Buttercup	Horse chestnut	Thorn apple
Horsetails	Russian knapweed	Yellow star thistle	Daffodil	Ivy	Yew
Jimsonweed	Tansy ragwort	Yew	Deadly nightshade	Laburnum	
Locoweed	Whitehead				

Fields must be safe and free from poisonous plants such as nightshades and ragwort (see above). Check your field every day to make sure that there are no dangers such as rabbit holes, broken fencing or rubbish.

Fencing

Not all types of fencing are safe for horses so look for posts and rails, hedging, electric, plastic or wire fencing designed specially for them. Barbed wire should never be used and can cause horrific injuries. Plain wire can be acceptable if kept fully taut, but wire fencing designed for other animals should be avoided.

Shelter

A field shelter or run-in barn will give protection from extremes of weather in both winter and summer. The front should be open and large enough to allow horses in and out without arguments, and the back should face the prevailing wind. If possible, the shelter should be sited on the highest ground, for best drainage.

Horses out for more than a very few hours need water and shelter facilities if they are not to become distressed in extremes of weather and possibly lose condition.

Company

Horses are herd animals and need company, preferably that of other horses or ponies. If this is impossible, try keeping your horse with other companions such as llamas, donkeys or goats. However, consult your veterinary surgeon before putting your horse in with other animals (especially a donkey) as you may need to take special worming precautions to protect your horse.

Management

You should check on your horse twice a day even if he lives out all the time. This is the only way in which you can deal quickly with any injuries or diseases and can make sure that there are no problems with fencing and water supplies.

Remember that removing your horse's droppings on alternate days during the grazing season goes a very long way towards keeping him (almost) parasite-free.

Wholesome pasture

Take a holistic view of managing your paddocks. Consult a specialist equine grass seed merchant and sow as wide a variety of beneficial grasses and herbs as possible. Be wary of natural water supplies, which can easily be polluted. Clean, mains water may be preferable, or ample rainwater.

Feeding

This is the single most important topic in horse management. Without a good diet your horse will not be healthy, feel at his best or be able to work optimally. Research continues to change feeding principles, but most horse owners seem reluctant to alter their traditional ways. It is important, though, to feed the horse like the animal he is – a herbivore evolved not only to survive but actually to thrive on rather poor grass.

Checklist
✓ the horse's digestion
✓ causes of colic
✓ importance of fibre
✓ essential nutrients
✓ grass and succulent foods
✓ feeding rules

The digestive system

The horse's digestive system is described on pages 34–35. The main points to remember are:

• The system is very sensitive and many horses are careful what they eat, bad food normally being rejected.

• Colic (see pages 184–185) can be caused by upset digestion triggered by stress, erratic feeding, insufficient fibre (bulk or roughage), too little water, changes in feeding (particularly hay and haylage), and some medicines and antibiotics.

• Feed as much quality fibre generally as the horse wants, and feed cereal concentrates and feeds made from them (cubes, nuts, pellets, coarse mixes and sweet feeds) only if absolutely essential, possibly on the advice of a vet or equine nutritionist.

Essential nutrients

A good, balanced diet is one that includes the correct proportions and amounts of all the following elements:

Water A young horse's body is made up of about 80 per cent water; in the adult horse this drops to about 60 per cent. Water loss can cause illness and even death. (See also pages 68–69.)

Carbohydrates These comprise sugar, starch and certain compounds within fibre. Some sugar is found in most foodstuffs. Molasses contains high levels of sugar as does fresh, young grass. Starch is found mainly in cereals.

Protein When broken down, proteins provide essential amino acids. These are used mainly for growth, pregnancy, milk production and repair of body tissues.

Fats and oils These are concentrated sources of energy, containing 2½ times as much energy as carbohydrates. Oil

Ponies should very rarely be fed cereal-based feeds unless a vet or nutritionist advises it. They do better on low-energy forage feeds.

is found in small quantities in most commercial foodstuffs and is often added (as vegetable oil) to the diets of hard-working horses.

Fibre Found in all feeds, particularly grass, hay, haylage and straw.

Minerals The major minerals are calcium, phosphorus, magnesium, potassium, sodium and chlorine; the main trace elements or minerals are copper, zinc, manganese, selenium and iron. The most important mineral balance is that of calcium to phosphorus: there should be more calcium than phosphorus in the diet, with a ratio of about 1½ parts calcium to 1 part phosphorus.

Vitamins Required in varying quantities to maintain health, helping to control chemical reactions and processes. The main vitamins are A, D, E, K and the B group. Green feeds are good sources, while hay and many cereals are low in vitamins and so a less important source.

Nature's feed

If your horse cannot graze, always give him plenty of succulent, juicy feeds day and night to compensate – such as carrots, apples, soaked sugar beet pulp and, if he will eat them, whole turnips, swedes, mangolds and fodder beets left in his stable. Hand-pulled grass should be welcome but do not feed short lawn clippings, which can clump together and cause colic. Graze your horse in hand as much as possible.

Modern rules of good feeding

The following rules imitate the horse's natural feeding habits to suit his digestive system.
• Allow the horse free and easy access to fresh, clean water at all times.
• Feed by weight according to the horse's type, constitution, temperament, workload, lifestyle and the varying weather.
• Feed any horse so that you cannot see his ribs but can feel them easily.
• Make fibre the main dietary staple, and give as many different types as you can (as in nature) all at the same time. Fit tubs in all four corners of the stable, on the floor, containing different forages (fibre feeds) – hay, haylage and short-chopped forages such as alfalfa.
• Do not feed your horse separate 'meals'. Scatter any cereals through his short-chopped forage so that he obtains tiny amounts all the time.
• Never leave your horse without fibre for several hours, such as overnight or while you are at work.
• All but the hardest-working horses can probably perform well on hay or haylage plus short-chopped alfalfa or forage mixes, plus a broad-spectrum (wide-ranging) vitamin and mineral supplement. Add soaked sugar beet pulp, carrots, apples and extra oil for those in hard work.
• Increase the work before increasing the feed and decrease the feed before decreasing the work. Overfeeding concentrates/cereals even slightly can cause circulatory and digestive problems. Increasing the work before increasing the feed means that the horse will be using up existing energy in his body before starting on an increased supply from a higher ration. Similarly, by decreasing the ration before reducing the work level, energy will not be stored and built up to excess in the body.

Get help

Make full use of the qualified equine nutritionists at the company whose feeds you use. They will be glad to help you devise a suitable diet for your horse or pony and most company helplines are free or charged at local rates. A vet interested in nutrition is also a great help.

• Make any changes to the diet over two weeks or more.
• Use only high-quality, clean feeds.
• Do not perform fast work immediately after feeding or feed immediately after hard work. After work, a horse's resources are being used to restore energy to his hard-worked muscles and to remove waste products. If you feed anything (fibre or concentrates) shortly after work, sufficient energy for digestion might not be available and the food could be improperly digested, or the horse could even get colic. Similarly, working a horse hard straight after eating could mean that energy is diverted from digestion to service the more immediate demands of muscle use, with the same results.

Most owners enjoy feeding their horses, but make sure you are feeding him what he needs and not making uninformed guesses.

Watering

Water is your horse's most important nutrient. A horse can live for a few weeks without food but for only a very few days without water. Next to fresh air, it is the thing he needs most to survive. A hard-working horse in hot weather can, and needs to, drink up to about 50 litres (11 gallons) of water a day. Years ago, water troughs were plentiful in towns for working horses, and some are still in use today.

Checklist
✓ importance of water
✓ causes of dehydration
✓ checking for dehydration
✓ when to give water
✓ containers: suitable and unsuitable

The importance of water

Water makes up most of a horse's bodyweight. Muscle tissue contains a lot of water but fat is just that and is lighter than water. This is why, when horses are being made fit for work, and their muscles increase in size, they often put on weight while slimming down (losing fat).

Dehydration

For various reasons, horses sometimes drink too little water and then become dehydrated, a serious condition that can need veterinary treatment.

Dehydration can be caused by a horse sweating too much:
• Perhaps you have worked your horse harder than you intended, or haven't noticed that his bucket is empty.
• Standing inside a stuffy, humid stable on a hot day can cause a horse to sweat so much that he begins to dehydrate.
• Standing inside a trailer or horsebox can have the same effect, so at competitions always try to park in the shade.
• Even being rugged up too much on a warm spring day can cause a horse to sweat profusely.

Dehydration occurs more easily on humid days. Normally, sweat evaporates into the surrounding air, carrying excess body heat with it and cooling the body. However, when the air itself is loaded with moisture the sweat cannot evaporate, the body does not cool, and the horse's sensors tell the sweat glands to work even harder and excrete more (liquid) sweat, the result being dehydration.

Checking for dehydration

Significantly dehydrated horses may feel too poorly to want to drink and will need veterinary help. Dehydration can kill

Water containers are best sited along the fence line in paddocks, not in the open where they create a possible obstruction to galloping.

horses quite quickly, so the situation is urgent. There are two good ways to check if your horse is dehydrated.

Skin pinch test This shows definite dehydration. Simply pick up a fold of skin between finger and thumb on the horse's neck just in front of the shoulder. When you let go it should fall flat within 1 second; if it doesn't, the horse is dehydrated.

Did you know

Dehydration in horses is just as likely in freezing weather as in hot weather, because water supplies may freeze over in fields and even in stables. Horses will not normally break ice on troughs themselves – you will need to break it for them several times a day, or in regions subject to extremes of temperature provide water in heated containers. A football floating on the top of a trough helps to prevent complete freezing, but not in extremely cold weather.

Capillary refill test This shows even slight dehydration. Press your thumb just above a front tooth on the gum to create a pale patch. The blood, and so the colour, should return to normal within 1.5 seconds; if it doesn't, the horse is dehydrated. The horse's gum may also become dry and tacky.

Watering rules

• It is safest to make sure that your horse has fresh, clean water with him at all times in both stable and field.
• When travelling, stop and offer him water every two hours on a long trip, and always before leaving and on arrival, plus during the day.
• It is wrong to withhold water for long before fast work. Allowing the horse to drink helps to ward off dehydration, so water should be removed only half an hour before starting hard work.
• It is also wrong to remove water at feed times. Drinking a little before, during and after eating helps digestion. Horses who have water always present do not drink long draughts, so no harm is done.

Containers

You can leave water with your horse in two separate corners in his stable, so that if he does a dropping in one the other should remain clean. Many people use tubs, which hold more water – but, because they can be heavy, this often results in their not being cleaned out daily, as they should be. Containers should be scrubbed every day in clear water. Baby sterilizer is suitable for disinfection, if necessary.

Horses prefer drinking from large containers at ground level. With the type of water source shown here, some horses do not drink enough.

What if my horse won't drink ?

If your horse won't drink it could be for one of the following reasons:
• His container may be too high, making it uncomfortable for him to drink. Automatic drinkers should have their tops no higher than the horse's elbow, as for mangers. Ideally, water should be placed at ground level.
• The water could be stale, dirty or contaminated with stable debris, dust or droppings. Change it frequently.
• Containers that rattle, smell, have become slimy or are too small and narrow put off many horses. A large, clean container is best, at a low level.
• If the horse is away from home, the local water may smell and taste strange. Take large camping containers of water with you.

Grooming

Field-kept and feral horses groom themselves by rubbing and rolling to help deter skin parasites, stimulate their skin, help remove old hairs and make themselves feel good. They rub each other with teeth and muzzles, concentrating on the forehand. This mutual grooming is probably involved in relationship bonding. If your horse tries to mutual groom you when you rub his withers, take it as a compliment.

Checklist
- ✓ why groom?
- ✓ checking the horse's body and shoes
- ✓ brushing over
- ✓ full grooming
- ✓ equipment

Reasons to groom

Grooming is one of the most rewarding jobs in looking after a horse. It is a great way to bond with him.

The grass-kept horse needs to be tidied up daily but not groomed too thoroughly (with the body brush or, indeed, washed) because the natural grease in his coat helps to keep him warm. Even in hot regions, there may be a considerable drop in temperature at night and most horses much prefer living out without a rug, except in very cold weather.

For stabled horses, however, grooming is an important and enjoyable part of their day – as long as the person grooming is neither too rough nor tickling them through too gentle a pressure.

Grooming also ensures you check every part of the horse, spotting any lumps, bites, abrasions and wounds that may need attention.

Quartering

This is a quick brush-over and tidy-up before the horse's work session.

1 Briskly but carefully use a dandy brush on the horse's body to remove dried urine and manure (stable stains), bedding, dried mud and sweat.

2 Brush the head, mane and tail with a body brush.

3 'Lay' the mane and top of the tail. Take a water brush and dip the tips only of the bristles into water. Shake the brush hard downwards to remove excess water and then brush over the mane from the roots and also over the top (dock) of the tail.

4 Pick out the feet with a hoofpick to remove debris and droppings. Check the feet and shoes at the same time.

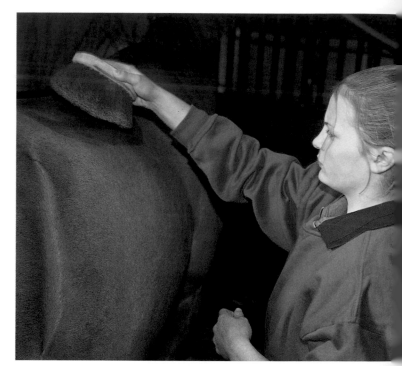

Good grooming helps to keep a horse comfortable and healthy.

To check if a shoe is loose

If a horse has a loose shoe, you will hear a clanking noise when he walks on a hard surface. Compare this to the firm 'clip-clop' sound of the other three hooves.

Check if you can fit the point of a hoofpick under the shoe at the heel and move it: if you can, the shoe is loose.

Basic grooming kit

1 Dandy mitt
2 Trimming scissors
3 Mane comb
4 Stable rubber
5 Rubber curry comb
6 Metal curry comb
7 Sponges
8 Body brush

Full grooming

This is done after work, when the horse had dried off and cooled down but is still warm. Grooming after work is easier because the skin is warm and supple and has been working hard. Sweat and natural oils have been secreted on to the hair, which lubricate it. These factors make body brushing very effective at this time, provided the horse has mostly dried off, as dirt is more easily removed.

1 Start by brushing off any dried mud and sweat. Work all over the horse, from front to back on both sides. Brush following the lie of the horse's coat. Depending on the degree of mud or dirt and the sensitivity of the horse's skin, you can start with a dandy brush, or rubber curry comb or curry glove.

2 Next use the body brush and metal curry comb (to clean the brush, never the horse). Lean your weight on the brush and make long, sweeping strokes along the lie of the coat, about six in one place. Then scrape the bristles over the teeth of the curry comb. Proceed all over the horse. Be careful on the head (where you may need to use just your hands) and legs, and under the belly. Be sensitive to where your horse is ticklish and work more gently.

3 Damp two sponges and carefully sponge clean the eyes, nostrils and lips with one, and the sheath or udder, around the anus, the vulva and under the tail with the other. Always keep them separate.

4 Pick out the horse's feet with a hoofpick.

5 Lay the mane and tail using a water brush.

6 Give the horse a final polish by bundling up your stable rubber or an old tea towel in your hand and flopping it all over him with the lie of the hair.

Clipping and trimming

Clipping removes the winter coat of working horses, so that they do not sweat excessively and become chilled after work. Some believe that horses 'sweat off' condition (weight) but there seems to be no scientific evidence for this. Trimming was devised to neaten up horses. Clipping and trimming are often overdone; it is better and more humane management to clip and trim as little as the horse's work requires.

Checklist
✓ why clip?
✓ clipping your horse
✓ types of clip
✓ trimming manes and tails
✓ trimming ears, jaw and fetlocks
✓ leave whiskers on

Which horses need clipping?

Horses that are going to sweat much in winter due to working need to be clipped, as do stabled horses that have naturally thick, greasy coats that would otherwise be impossible to keep clean. It is certainly not kind to clip a fine-coated, thin-skinned horse that is not working particularly hard. Rugs do not replace the coat completely and, it appears, are uncomfortable to most horses unless they fit exceptionally well.

Clipping your horse

Most owners feel that it is less trouble to call in a professional. Your horse must be clean and dry for the blades to cut cleanly, otherwise they will blunt, pull the hair and your horse could become difficult to clip.

Trimming

This involves trimming excess hair off the forelock, mane and tail, the fetlocks, under the jaw, and from the outsides of the fronts of the ears.

Shortening mane and forelock hair Hold the ends between thumb and finger and quickly snap the hair off sideways. This is not allowed in some breed showing classes.

Pulling a mane Back-comb the hair up to the roots with a mane comb until the longest hairs are left in the fingers of your other hand. Then press your thumb against the comb at their roots and quickly pull out a very few hairs – about six at most. Instruction and practise will make you proficient. Humane trimming combs are available that make the job easier.

Pulling a tail This involves pulling out the hairs from the

Ears and whiskers

Never trim the hair from the insides of your horse's ears. It is important for catching dirt and debris that might otherwise fall inside the ear.

Never remove the long whiskers (vibrissae) around your horse's eyes and muzzle. They act like antennae that he uses for feeling around and are an important part of his sensory equipment.

Do not be seduced by the idea that your horse will 'look better' with either of these removed.

sides of the dock to give a tapered appearance. Simply wrap two or three hairs around your fingers and pull them sharply down and out.

Banging a tail This is done with very sharp shears. Close your hand right around all the hairs at the end of the dock and run it down the tail to a little lower than you want the tail to be – mid-cannon length suits most horses. Keep a steady downward pull on the hair. Position the scissors above your hand, pointing them directly between the horse's hindlegs and slightly upwards. Make a single bold snip and let go. This method ensures that the bottom of the tail is level when your horse or pony raises it in movement.

Trimming the ears, jaw and fetlocks You will need a small wide-toothed comb and a pair of sharp, curved fetlock scissors. Hold the edges of the ears together and carefully snip off the hair that protrudes, plus any tufts at the bottom. For jaw and fetlocks, comb the hair up against its lie and snip off the hairs between the teeth of the comb.

This is a blanket clip. It is suitable for almost any horse in hard work.

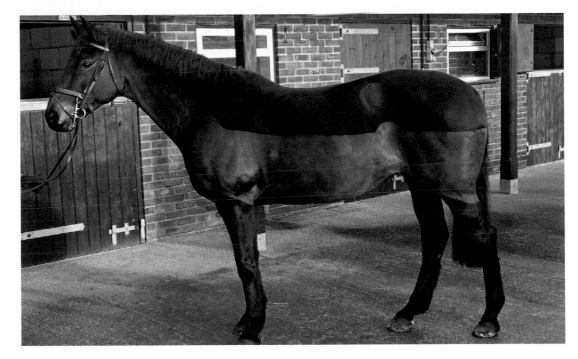

This is a chaser clip, named after steeplechasers who are often clipped this way. It is suitable for fine-coated and thin-skinned horses in hard work during winter.

Types of clip

There are variations of these clips, but the following are the basic styles:

Full clip All the body hair is removed.

Hunter clip All the hair except the legs and a saddle-shaped patch on the back is removed.

Blanket clip Hair is left on the legs and a patch the shape of a folded blanket over the back and hindquarters, with the rest of the hair being removed.

Chaser clip Like a blanket clip, but with the hair left on the upper half of the neck up to the ears.

Trace clip The hair is removed only from the underneath of the neck, the chest and the lower half of the body, plus around the tops of the legs.

Irish clip Similar to a trace clip, but the hair is left on around the tops of the hindlegs.

Bib clip The hair is removed in the shape of a bib on the horse's chest and usually up the underside of the neck.

Daily foot care

Looking after your horse's feet properly every day is one of the most important things you can do to keep him comfortable, healthy and sound. You cannot ride a horse that has uncomfortable or sore feet, and although you cannot shoe him yourself, you can help to ensure that his feet remain in good condition.

Checklist

✓ foot structure
✓ how to pick out feet
✓ checking feet and shoes
✓ why shoes?
✓ using hoof oil

Structure of the foot

The part of the foot we see from the outside, the wall, consists of horn like our own fingernails. On the inside of the foot, there is a complex mesh of sensitive tissue and blood vessels, which binds the outside of the pedal (foot) bone inside the hoof (which gives it its shape) to the inside of the horny wall.

Underneath the foot, you will see a triangular wedge of softer, rubbery horn extending forward from the heels towards the toe. Called the frog, this helps to stop the horse slipping (although shoeing interferes with this action) and is part of the blood-pumping mechanism that maintains a healthy circulation within the foot and up the lower part of the leg.

The arched area between the frog and the bearing surface of the wall (the outer rim that touches the ground or to which the shoe is nailed) is called the sole. This is of thinner horn and horses can bruise their feet if the sole receives much pressure from, say, a stone.

Foot tip

Do not use ordinary, old-fashioned hoof oils on your horse's hooves. Oil can interfere with the horn's ability to 'breathe' and to regulate the hoof's water intake. Dry, brittle hooves are usually more in need of water than oil. The best way to ensure healthy horn growth is to feed a diet with the correct balance of vitamins and minerals.

Did you know ?

It can take up to a year for a horse's foot to grow down from the coronet (the raised band at the top of the hoof that produces the hoof horn) to the ground at the toe or front of the foot, less at the heels or back of the foot.

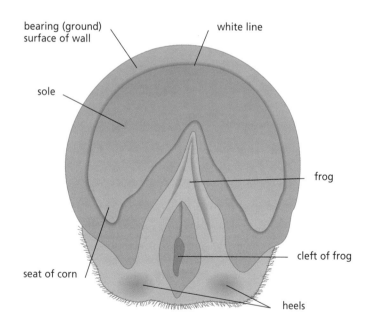

Picking out the feet

Because the underside of the foot is not smooth and level, it is easy for manure, dirt and other debris to lodge in it and make the feet uncomfortable. Also, if the underside of the foot is never exposed to air because of packed-in dirt, an

Picking out the feet thoroughly at least once every day is one of the horse owner's most important jobs.

unpleasant and stubborn disease called thrush can infect the frog and even, in bad cases, penetrate the horn to the sensitive, inner parts of the foot. Cleaning out at least once a day and preferably more is, therefore, an important part of your daily routine.

1 Pick out the underneath of the foot thoroughly using a hoofpick, working from heel to toe and making sure that all dirt, stones and other debris is removed.

2 Check the condition of the horn – if it is soft or smelly there could be a problem.

3 Check that the shoes are fixed on securely. The nail clenches (turned-over nail ends that hold the shoe to the foot) on the hoof wall should be flush with the horn and if you put the tip of your hoofpick under the shoe at the heel it should be firm, not loose. Horses with loose shoes cannot be ridden.

Why do horses need to be shod?

When people began working horses, they realized that the horn of their feet was wearing down quicker than it could grow and the horses were becoming footsore. The hooves needed protection, and the solution was shoes.

Today, most horses are shod, but those with hard, tough feet working mainly on soft or smooth hard going can manage very well without shoes – and, some say, better than if they were shod.

Hoof oil or not?

Standard hoof oil is not recommended except for occasional shows or other special events. This is because it can seal the hoof and interfere with the natural moisture balance of the horn, which may become weak and soft if hoof oil is used regularly. If you are concerned about the condition of your horse's feet, discuss this with your farrier or vet.

Complementary therapies

Many therapies have been used for thousands of years but, with the advent of modern antibiotics, anti-inflammatories, painkillers and other drugs, natural therapies became less popular. They are now of great interest again, and can be used alone or with orthodox veterinary treatments, as well as in health maintenance. Here we give an overview of some of the most prominent therapies.

Checklist
✓ therapies to choose
✓ advice from your vet
✓ professional practitioners
✓ doing it yourself

Aromatherapy

Aromatherapy uses essential oils from plants, which are usually inhaled or diluted in a carrier or base oil and rubbed into the skin. Never give oils to your horse by mouth except on the advice of a professional therapist, usually working on veterinary referral, according to your national laws.

Identifying the right oil for both the horse and the problem (psychological or physical) involves looking up the uses of each oil, selecting likely sounding ones, then offering each bottle in turn for the horse to smell. Keep the top of the bottle inside your fist, level with the top of your hand. If he shows interest and even tries to lick the bottle, he needs this essential oil.

A therapist will show you how to dilute and blend essential oils in a base oil, as most are too concentrated to use 'neat'. They will also show you how to use them.

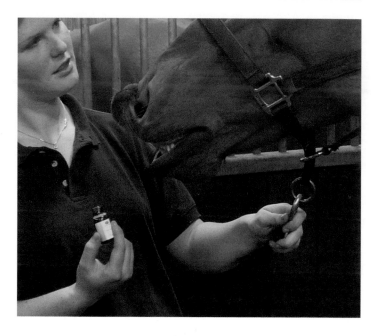

This horse is performing the 'flehmen' action, raising his top lip so that he can savour the aroma.

Flower remedies and essences

Flower essences are produced worldwide, the best known being Bach Flower Remedies. They are entirely safe for horses, humans and other animals. You need to know your horse well so that you can choose an appropriate remedy from the guide booklet, according to his personality and disorder. The remedies are liquid and are usually administered into the side of the mouth from a dropper four or more times a day.

Herbalism

Herbalism is the oldest form of natural therapy. In the wild, horses practise their own form of herbal medicine, having 'nutritional intuition' about what they need.

Modern herbicides, weed killers and even fertilizers have eliminated most herbs from domestic paddocks. Now, however, as their uses are once again being recognized, herb strips are being sown by the more conscientious and knowledgeable landowners.

You can also buy herbal products as feed supplements from good retailers, although it is advisable to ring the manufacturer's helpline, speak to a herbalist and get advice on what to use. Many are also available as lotions and creams for external use.

Homoeopathy

Homoeopathy is not the same as herbalism, although plants are used as remedies along with inorganic substances. It was used by the ancient Greeks, but modern homoeopathy was refined by Samuel Hahnemann (d. 1843), who believed that every living thing has a vital life force or energy. When this energy is unbalanced, illness occurs.

Homoeopathic remedies are prepared using increasing dilutions until no molecules (particles) of the remedy itself remain, only the energy it gives off. This is believed to work with the body's energy to balance it and stimulate the body to help itself.

Homoeopathy works on the principle that a substance that can cause specific symptoms in a healthy body can alleviate them in a sick one. The most famous example of this is malaria. If a healthy person takes chinchona (quinine) they develop malaria-like symptoms, yet the same substance alleviates the symptoms in a person suffering from the disease.

Massage and hand rubbing

Massage originated in ancient China and, like many other therapies, worked originally on the basis of stimulating and balancing the body's life force or energy. You can start by running your hands over your horse and feeling where muscles are tight, or noting reaction to soreness. When you sense a problem area, use your intuition to massage and rub the area gently. Gradually move to surrounding areas until the tissues relax.

Hand rubbing was a daily part of a thorough grooming routine for past generations. It releases tension and makes hard-worked muscles feel better, promoting blood and lymph circulation.

Herbal medicines

Although they may give good results, do not expect miracle cures from over-the-counter proprietary products. They generally include only the safest and mildest herbs, and will not be tailored to the individual horse's needs. Always consult a vet if you are unsure whether a particular herbal product is suitable for your horse, and perhaps ask for a referral to a medical herbalist.

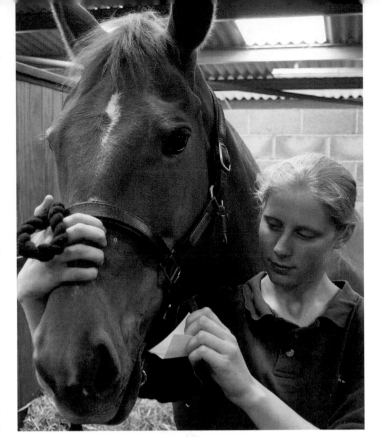

Do not touch the homoeopathic remedies yourself as this reduces their energy. Tip the pill or powder into a paper chute, then into the horse's mouth.

Professional therapists

One of the easiest ways to find details of administrative organizations for complementary therapists is via the internet. Another way is by word of mouth. You can also ask any good bookshop to find out which books are available on the therapy you have in mind. Such books nearly always give the address of the therapy's administrative body or registration council. Your local reference library should also be able to help you or, of course, your vet or phone book.

Any conscientious and realistic professional therapist will know that, although insurance policies sometimes cover their fees, many owners cannot afford regular consultations. The best are usually willing to show owners how to use their therapy at a basic level, with top-up consultations as required.

Tellington Touch

The Tellington Touch Equine Awareness Method (TTEAM) was devised by Canadian Linda Tellington-Jones and is a complete remedial system of riding, ground training and bodywork (the latter being called the TTouch, pronounced Tee Touch). Linda Tellington-Jones has written several books on the system and qualifies practitioners in the method. It is also very suitable for owner application.

Saddles, pads and numnahs

Saddles were invented to make long rides more comfortable for the rider and to help him stay on during active riding such as herding and fighting. Today, we use horses for many other purposes and we have various 'seats' or styles of riding, which are usually helped by a saddle designed specifically to position the rider best for that sport. What are the basic designs and equipment you need to know about?

Checklist

✓ types of saddle
✓ pads and numnahs
✓ girths, stirrups and leathers
✓ looking after tack

General purpose saddle

The general purpose saddle is the most useful for riders who want to do a bit of everything, including jumping. They may have different names according to the manufacturer, but if you ask for a GP saddle (as they are known) they will know what you want.

This type of saddle is made so that the framework on which it is built (called the tree) has the front arch (pommel) tilted back slightly at the top and forward at the bottom (the points), with the stirrup bars over which the stirrup leathers hang set a little way behind them. This allows the rider to adopt a seat with the upper body slightly forward for jumping quite easily. The flap on which the rider's leg rests is styled ('cut') moderately forward to accommodate the knee.

Dressage saddle

If you do not want to jump at all, you may prefer a dressage saddle. There are many types available and, as with all saddles, you need to try a few to find one that suits you. The flap is straighter cut and the stirrup bars set a little further back than on a GP saddle, to allow for the longer stirrup length and upright seat (riding position) used for flatwork (non-jumping riding) and competitive dressage.

Jumping saddle

Specialist jumping saddles have the flaps more forward cut than a GP saddle to accommodate a shorter stirrup length. Most people find them a little uncomfortable for ordinary riding on the flat, hacking and so on.

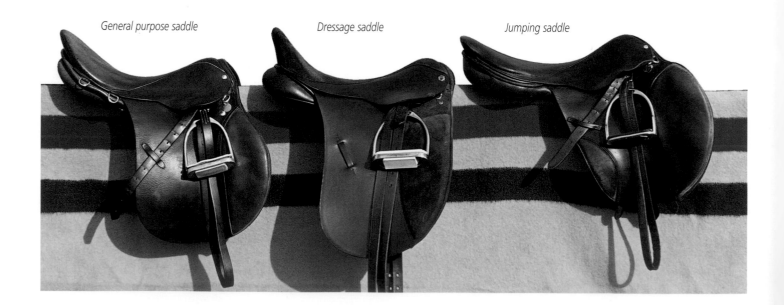

General purpose saddle   *Dressage saddle*   *Jumping saddle*

A numnah with a loop at the bottom for the girth to pass through. The straps further up fold back around the girth straps on the saddle.

Saddle pads

Although saddlers maintain that a well-fitting saddle is not helped by a pad, most people use them, believing that they add comfort and absorb sweat. They are rectangular, usually padded in various ways, and have loops to thread over the girth and sometimes the stirrup leathers to help keep them in position. You should choose a design with a rise at the front to accommodate the horse's withers.

Numnahs

An Indian word, this is a saddle-shaped pad that, again, should be cut to accommodate the withers. As with a saddle pad, there will probably be loops to help prevent the numnah slipping backwards during use.

It is a good idea to choose a girth that is 'cut away' (shaped back) behind the elbows to allow room for the horse's forelegs to move in comfort. Girths that dig in behind the elbows are uncomfortable for the horse and can prevent him moving freely and correctly.

Stirrups and leathers

Stirrups are best made from heavy metal, stainless steel being strong and easy to clean. There are various safety designs. You can buy rubber treads to slot into the bottom of the stirrups to help your foot stay put. Synthetic stirrups can be useful if you suffer from stiffness in your knees or ankles, as they have a little 'give'.

The slot, or eye, at the top of the stirrup is for the leather to pass through, so your leathers must be narrow enough to do this but wide enough to be comfortable against your shin.

Take care

Saddles are very expensive and fairly fragile. If you drop your saddle or throw it down, you can easily break the tree and it will be ruined. Always stand your saddle on its pommel on a non-scratch surface: bring the girth over the top of the saddle covering the pommel and cantle (rear arch), then prop it on the pommel (on the girth fabric) and lean the cantle (also protected by the girth) against the wall. Alternatively, temporarily put it over a fence or on a bale of straw. If you put it on the top of your horse's door, he may chew and mark it.

Tack cleaning

Synthetic tack can usually be cleaned easily in accordance with the maker's instructions but leather tack requires more care, although specially treated leather may not need conventional cleaning.

1 Wash leather tack with a moist sponge dipped in lukewarm water to remove sweat and dirt. For very dirty items, add a few drops only of washing-up liquid to a bucket of water.

2 Rub a dressing of saddle soap or a proprietary dressing (follow the instructions) into the leather to protect it. With saddle soap, take a different, damp sponge and rub it firmly on to the soap, then rub it firmly in circular movements well into the leather.

3 Wrap the saddle-soap sponge around straps and run it up and down them. Poke excess soap out of buckle holes with a matchstick or similar.

4 Do not get soap or metal polish on to the bit, as the taste can remain and is horrible for the horse. Wash metal items like bits and stirrups in hand-hot, clear water. Clean buckles and stirrups with metal polish, removing any polish from the leather immediately.

Did you know ?

Most back problems in horses are caused by badly fitting saddles. Such a saddle can injure your horse's back and cause all kinds of problems in riding, handling and the horse's use of his own body – for example, in lying down, scratching himself and so on. Make sure that you have your saddle properly fitted by a qualified saddle fitter.

How a saddle should fit

Saddle fitting is a skilled profession whose importance is understood by conscientious owners. Owners should acquire a working knowledge of it from any good book on tack. Many problems in riding and equine behaviour are caused by badly fitting saddles. Horses' weight and shape vary depending on diet and work, so saddles should be checked for fit before a season's work, or twice yearly if the horse is in permanent work.

Checklist
- ✓ importance of correct fitting
- ✓ the saddle tree
- ✓ allowing for movement
- ✓ saddle width
- ✓ faults in fitting

Tree width

Any saddle must fit well: if it pinches, rocks, rubs or bangs on the horse's back it will cause pain and maybe permanent damage. The basis of a good fit depends on the tree (the saddle's frame) being the correct width for the horse. An expert fitter will advise you and should be able to adjust the saddle's stuffing to give the best weight distribution – *if* the tree is the right width in the first place.

Basic points

A saddle should:
- sit centrally
- have a clear channel of daylight from pommel to cantle, so that it does not press on the withers or spine
- not interfere with the shoulders
- not rub the loins
- not cause uneven pressure anywhere on the back.

Freedom of the shoulders

When the horse extends his foreleg, the shoulder blade rotates around a point about one-third of the way down it from the wither. The top part moves backwards and the lower part (the point of the shoulder) moves forwards.

If the top part of the shoulder blade contacts the front edge of the saddle every time it moves backwards, the horse will experience pressure, discomfort, restriction and maybe bruising. The saddle will also be lifted slightly by the shoulder blade on each side with the movement of the forelegs and shoulders, making it rock from side to side. This can bruise the back and create an unstable base for the rider's seat.

Save your cash

The most prestigious and expensive saddles may not be the best for your horse. What matters is having a saddle that really fits your horse like a glove, not to support an upmarket logo.

You must be able to fit the width of the little-finger (outside) edge of your hand between the front of the saddle and the top of the horse's shoulder blade (immediately below the withers) *when the foreleg is fully extended.*

Width

At the back, the panel beneath the cantle must not extend further back than the horse's last rib. You must be able to fit the width of three fingers between the pommel and the withers when the horse's heaviest rider is leaning forward, and the same beneath the cantle when they are leaning back – any more and the saddle could be too narrow, any less and it could be too wide.

Bridging and pressure

Many saddles today are made with a rather flat panel beneath the seat, which causes them to 'bridge' the back, creating pressure in front and behind but not fully contacting the in-between area. This is a serious fault that causes hollowing of the horse's back due to the inevitable discomfort.

Some saddles press in under the cantle and some (usually those that are too narrow) cause pressure below and behind

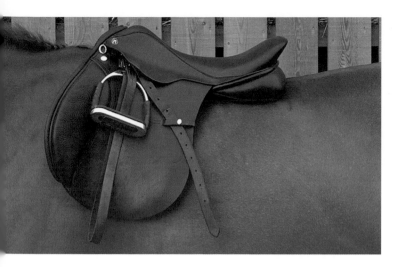

This saddle is too far forward and will interfere with the action of the shoulders. It is tilted upwards at the front, so the rider will slide out of balance, and sit badly.

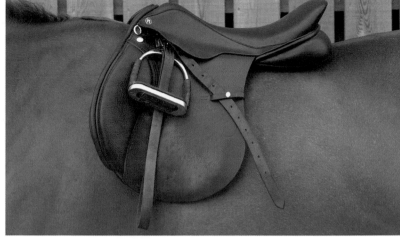

This saddle is correctly positioned, leaving the shoulders and loins free.

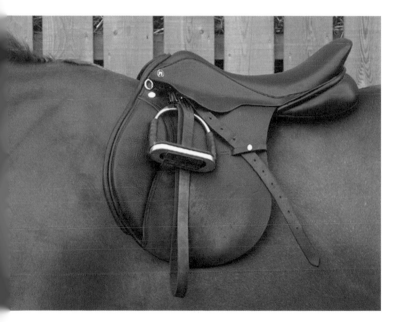

This saddle is too far back so, although the shoulders are free, it is pressing on the sensitive loin area.

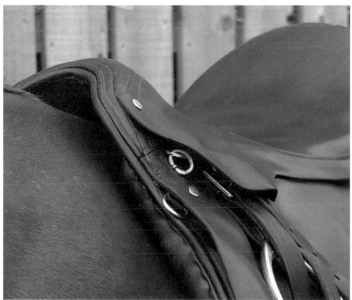

This saddle seems to be a good fit – the correct width and room above the withers – but it will sink down, possibly pressing on them, under a rider's weight.

the withers, even to the extent that hollows form there due to restriction of blood supply and atrophy of muscle tissue – a serious fault indeed.

Be prepared to ride

It is not possible to judge saddle fit solely on a standing horse. The saddle fitter will need to see the horse ridden by his heaviest rider.

There are two of you to consider

The panels (under the seat) of your saddle should fit your horse and the seat should fit you. If the saddle's length fits your horse but is too short for your seat, then you need a saddle with a longer seat.

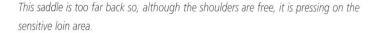

Saddling up and unsaddling

Many horses regard saddling up with trepidation and resignation but they should not expect discomfort during saddling up. It should be done considerately and with knowledge, otherwise it can upset the horse before you start. It can also tell you a lot about the horse's physical and mental states.

Checklist
✓ position the saddle correctly
✓ girth up gradually
✓ be considerate throughout
✓ unsaddling procedure

Saddle position

Do not place your saddle so far forward that it interferes with the movement of the horse's shoulder. Run your hand down under the front of the saddle to make sure that it is behind the movable shoulder blade and so will not impede its action.

Similarly, do not place it so far back that it presses on the loins. The back of the saddle should be no further back than the horse's last rib, which you can feel for.

Anatomy of a saddle

Saddles are built around a frame called a 'tree' made of wood (usually beech) and tempered steel (the 'spring'). A normal saddle will contain the following elements:

1	Cantle	6	Saddle pad
2	Seat	7	Saddle flap
3	Waist	8	Girth
4	Pommel	9	Panel
5	Skirt		

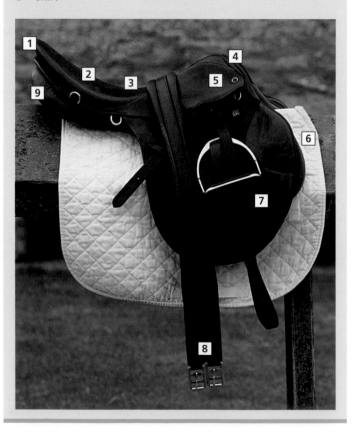

Your horse's reactions

If you horse looks worried, tosses his head, moves away from you or looks cross or even aggressive (ears back, nostrils wrinkled up and back), you know that he has had a bad time during saddling up. You should be as considerate and gentle as possible while still getting the job done. You can get him to associate the process with good things by giving him a titbit at both start and finish, taking your time, and considering how *you* would feel about the whole procedure being done to you.

Your first duty, though, is to ask your vet to check whether he is in pain, and call a saddle fitter to check the saddle and girth.

Saddling up

1 *Place the numnah or saddle pad on the horse's back near the wither and slide it into position along the lie of the coat. Check that it is not wrinkled on either side; if this goes unnoticed, it can cause a pressure rub.*

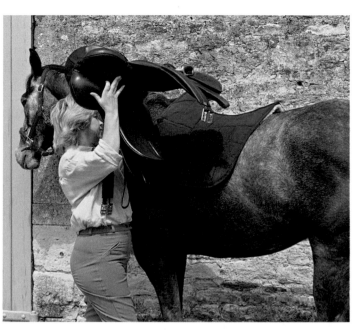

2 *Take the saddle with the girth attached on the off (right) side and place it carefully on top of the numnah or pad, easing it gently back into position.*

3 *Pick up the numnah or pad beneath the pommel and cantle with both hands and pull it well up into the saddle's gullet (beneath the seat, between the panels). This will help to prevent pressure on the horse's spine and, particularly, the withers, when the girth is tightened and during riding.*

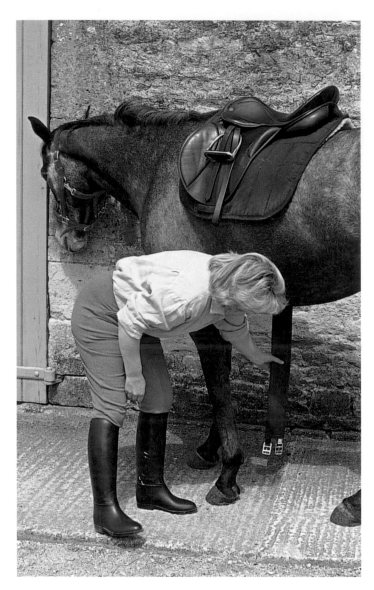

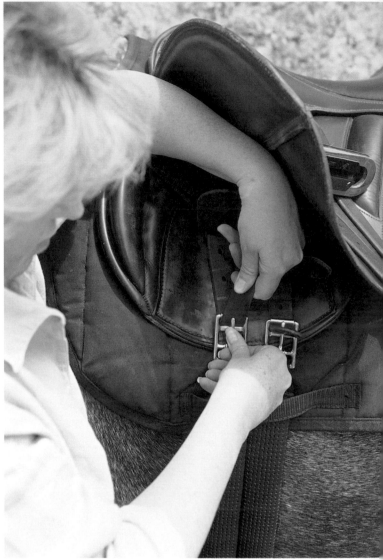

4 *Girthing up probably causes more resentment in horses than any other aspect of saddling up. Lift the girth and quietly drop the unattached end over the saddle, so that it hangs down on the off side. With nervous horses, walk around to the off side and lift the girth down. Check that it is buckled on the bottom hole of the girth tabs (straps). Return to the near (left) side, bend down and bring the girth under the horse's belly.*

5 *Gently buckle the girth on to the bottom hole on the girth tabs under the saddle flap, talking to your horse as you do so. Check that the numnah or pad is still well up in the gullet. While the horse is getting used to the touch of the girth, you can put on the bridle (see pages 92–93). Gradually tighten the girth alternately on the near and off sides until it is tight enough for you to mount. You should be able to slide the flat of four fingers between the girth and the horse, but should not be able to pull the girth away from his side.*

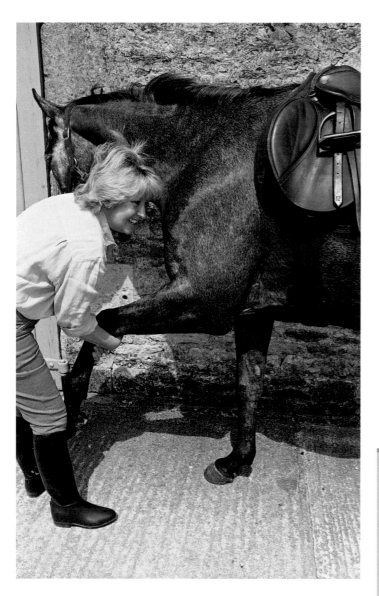

6 *At this point, gently lift the horse's near foreleg at the knee and stretch it forward, to ensure that no folds of skin are caught between the elbow and girth. Repeat on the off side. Finally, check that everything is in the correct place – and mount.*

Removing the saddle

When you dismount, speak to your horse and make a fuss of him. Most horses seem to appreciate this.

1 Lift the saddle flap on the near side and unbuckle the girth, making sure it does not drop and hit the horse's leg, which is most inconsiderate. Lift the saddle and pad or numnah together up off the horse's back, then bring them sideways towards you. Do not drag everything off the back.

2 Pick up the girth as it is coming over the horse's back and lay it on the seat, sweaty side downwards so that mud does not scratch the leather of the seat, as you slide everything off the horse.

3 Finally, rub the horse's back and girth area briskly with your hands to help restore the circulation, not forgetting the area directly under the breastbone.

Top tip

Girthing up can be particularly uncomfortable for the horse so do it very gradually as described above, one hole at a time over a few minutes. Have a friend to give your horse titbits as you do so. This has been scientifically proven to distract the horse from bad memories and associate girthing up (or any worrisome process) with pleasure and good things (titbits). Talk calmly and firmly to the horse to reassure him, but don't back off unless you experience outright aggression. If you do, seek professional help but never let anyone get rough with your horse.

Bridles and nosebands

We see many 'natural horsemen' today riding horses without bridles and bits. Working donkeys in developing countries also work this way, carrying their riders and/or burdens wearing no headgear. If this is possible, why use bridles? In most western societies involving motorized traffic and other risky situations, a bridle makes it likely that you will have good control should an 'incident' occur, so it is a safety precaution.

Checklist
- ✓ bridle styles
- ✓ parts of the bridle
- ✓ noseband designs
- ✓ bitless options

Bridle designs

The whole point of a bridle is to give the rider control of the horse's head. To this end, it must stay on.

English-style bridles

English-style bridles start with a headpiece passing behind the ears. Just below the ears, it splits (on each side) forming two cheekpieces that run down the sides of the horse's face. They have holes in them for buckling on two shorter straps (the bottom parts of the cheekpieces) to which the bit fastens to hold it up in the mouth. This arrangement makes it possible for you to adjust the length of the cheekpieces and thereby the height of the bit in the horse's mouth.

The second, narrower strap extending from the split is the throatlatch (pronounced 'throatlash'), which passes

Browbands

Browbands are often quite decorative, particularly those designed for showing. Western bridles (and saddles) have 'tooled' or carved patterns on leatherwork and metal, sometimes silver, ornaments. English browbands may be padded and have stitched patterns although hunters have plain leather. Some browbands have coloured strips of plastic wound around them. Velvet is used for show Hacks, Riding Horses and children's show ponies. The colours can be those of the stable, or to complement the horse's colouring.

Having a bridle put on must be a slightly uncomfortable procedure. Put yourself in your horse's place and be gentle and careful.

under the throat and fastens on the left side to help keep the whole bridle in place. There is also a strap passing around the horse's forehead, called the browband. This has loops at each end through which thread the cheekpieces and throatlatch. The reins fasten to the bit.

On English-style bridles with two bits, known as double bridles (see pages 88–89), there is another fitting or

Some Western bridles have no browband, although this one has. The horse is wearing a breast plate to help keep the heavy saddle in place.

headstall passing under the headpiece. This is to hold up the second bit. Obviously, such bridles have two sets of reins.

Some bridles from the classical academies such as the Spanish Riding School of Vienna do not always have throatlatches.

Western-style bridles

Most Western bridles consist of a headpiece, two cheekpieces and the browband, although some types have two slits in the headpiece through which the ears go, so a browband is not necessary. The throatlatch may be a separate loop of leather passing behind the headpiece and under the throat, kept in place by the loops on the ends of the browband.

Bitless bridles

The earliest bridles were just ropes passed around the horse's head and there were no bits. Later on, riders threaded strips of rawhide or jute rope through the horse's mouth, for extra control. Bitless bridles are still popular today, particularly among showjumpers and some endurance riders.

Bitless bridles are useful on some horses. They work on nose pressure, and some include poll pressure, too. Such bridles must be used with just as much care as the conventional bitted bridle.

Western riders often train their young horses in bitless bridles before graduating to specialist curb bits. These may look severe, but Western riders rely on balance and neck-reining (sideways pressure from the rein on the horse's neck), using a loose rein or the lightest possible contact with the horse's mouth.

Nosebands

The noseband can affect the action of the bit, and if adjusted too tightly can cause the horse a lot of discomfort and interfere with his breathing – horses are unable to breathe through their mouths. A good rider and well-schooled horse should not need a noseband.

Cavesson noseband This is simply a strap around the centre of the upper and lower jawbones. Many people think it makes the horse's head look smarter. It can also be used to attach a device called a standing martingale, to prevent certain horses putting their heads up beyond the point of the rider's control.

Flash noseband This noseband resembles a cavesson but has a second, narrow strap that fastens below the bit. This helps to keep the bit central and steady, and discourages the horse from opening his mouth too wide.

Grakle or cross-over noseband This looks like a cross or figure of eight and gives extra control by discouraging the horse from opening his mouth and crossing his jaw.

Drop noseband Not seen so often today, this noseband passes below the bit with the front strap at least 8cm (3in) above the nostrils. It can be a very severe noseband and must not be at all tight.

When using any noseband that passes below the bit, such as a flash or grakle, remember that you are not trying to strap the horse's mouth shut, which is very bad horsemanship.

Reins

The main difference between Western and English reins is that Western reins do not buckle together at their ends but remain as two separate pieces of leather. This is because Western horses are usually trained to 'ground tie': when the rider drops the reins (which fall easily to the ground, being separate), the horse knows to stand still. In English-style riding, this is not commonly taught and the reins buckle together so that, if the rider accidentally lets go, the reins remain on the horse's neck and are easy to pick up again.

Bits

Iron bits 4,000 years old have been found in eastern Asia, and early bits were also made from horn and bone. Most riders feel safer using a bit but if a horse really wants to go no bit will stop him. Most horses, though, are more controllable with a bit. There are hundreds of designs and the old saying that 'most bits are made for men's heads, not horses' mouths' is true. The horse may not agree with our choice of bit for him!

Checklist

✓ the simple snaffle
✓ curb bits
✓ gags
✓ bitting systems
✓ choose a mild bit
✓ your hands are more important than the bit

The snaffle

This is the simplest, most popular bit. Snaffles are available in many designs and the basic mouthpiece types are the straight-bar, mullen-mouth or half-moon shape, single-jointed and double-jointed snaffles. A straight-bar bit puts pressure on the tongue and is quite uncomfortable. Most horses go better in the mullen-mouthed sort. The single-jointed bit has a squeezing action (often called a 'nutcracker' action) and some horses go well in this.

Most, though, prefer a double-jointed bit such as the French link snaffle. This has a kidney-shaped central link that reduces the nutcracker effect and is more comfortable. The French link snaffle should not be confused with the Dr Bristol, which is often used on strong-pulling horses and has a flat-sided, central plate, which is angled so that the edge presses into the tongue, supposedly to discourage the horse from pulling.

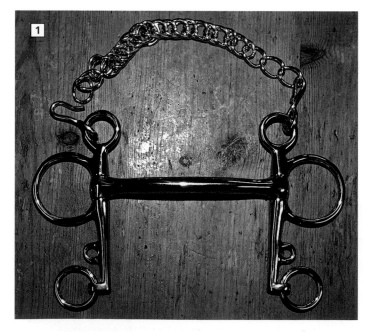

1 A mullen-mouthed or half-moon, stainless steel pelham

2 A single-jointed, stainless steel, eggbutt snaffle

3 A loose-ring, stainless steel, French link snaffle

Equine fact

Although bits are interesting and important, remember that what really matters is the skill with which you use them. Although control is important, most horses become harder to control, not easier, if they experience significant discomfort or pain, and it is bad horsemanship to hurt a horse intentionally.

The ends of the mouthpiece may be different types of ring or cheeks (metal vertical bars of various designs). A loose ring that slides through the ends of the mouthpiece gives a movable feel in the mouth, while the 'eggbutt' and D-ring are fixed so that the bit moves less. Full cheeks can help with steering on a young horse.

The mouthpiece can be made from stainless steel, rubber-covered metal, various metal alloys or special plastics. Some people think that copper, sweet-iron and other bits with a 'taste' are pleasurable to the horse and encourage him to salivate and accept the bit. However, excessive salivation can actually be a result of distress in mammals, as is excessive mouthing of the bit in horses – and how do we know that a horse really likes the taste of a bit we have chosen for him and that he cannot remove? It is probably more sensible to use tasteless stainless steel or plastic, and give the horse a mint for a pleasant taste before and after putting in the bit.

The double bridle

This is the most sophisticated bitting system, and allows a good rider to use delicate aids on a schooled horse to produce fine adjustments to the way he carries himself. It should not be used by inexperienced riders or on unschooled horses.

The double bridle has two bits, each with separate reins: the bridoon resembles a thin snaffle and fits above a curb bit (rather like a letter H with the central bar slightly higher), which is used with a curb chain that fits into the curb or chin groove just above the horse's fleshy chin. This works on leverage and must be used very carefully.

The pelham

This bit reproduces the action of the double bridle in one mouthpiece that has two sets of rings for the reins. Although less subtle, many horses work well in pelhams and they can give greater control than snaffles. The pelham should ideally be used with two pairs of reins (those on the bottom ring of the bit cheekpiece giving greater leverage), but some riders prefer to fit leather roundings to the bridoon and curb rings, and attach a single rein to these.

The kimblewick (kimberwick)

Similar to the pelham is the kimblewick. This bit is fitted with a curb chain but has a single D-shaped ring at either end of the mouthpiece and is used with a single rein. It exerts little leverage, but is stronger than a snaffle and some horses go well in it.

Gags

A commonly used bit is the Dutch gag or European gag. This normally has a single-jointed mouthpiece and a ring set on top of the main bit ring for the cheekpieces. Below the main bit ring are two more for the reins, giving different degrees of leverage like a curb (although there is no chain). Combined with the ring for the cheekpieces, this makes for significant poll pressure and an upward, 'gag' effect from the mouthpiece. This is a strong bit that, insensitively used, can ruin a horse's mouth.

The so-called American gag has a curved sidepiece with rings or slots on the top and bottom for the cheekpieces and reins respectively, although the reins can also be fastened level with the mouthpiece. This gives variable leverage and, again, can be a powerful bit.

Special bit systems

There are several proprietary bitting systems such as the Nathe, KK and Myler systems, which are beyond the scope of this book but are well worth looking into.

Did you know...?

Horses that produce a lot of froth around their mouths during work are probably uncomfortable, distressed and even angry. Although a horse needs a moist mouth for the bit to feel comfortable and movable in his mouth, excessive saliva and froth indicate irritation and even pain.

How a bridle should fit

If your bridle and bit do not fit your horse and feel comfortable to him, he will not work well and may become difficult, which can cause control problems. Deliberately causing a horse discomfort or pain in this way is surely cruel. Today many bridles seem to be fitted too tightly, and many bits do not fit well and are adjusted too high in the mouth. Here, we explain how to fit a bridle and bit properly – and comfortably.

Checklist

✓ fitting each piece
✓ bit fit
✓ curb chains
✓ reins should be long enough
✓ do not cause discomfort

The headpiece and browband of this bridle fit well but the throatlatch is too tight. The bit is a reasonable height, creating one wrinkle at the corner of the mouth.

Bridle fit

As a basic rule, you should be able to slide a finger easily under all the straps against your horse's head. If you can't, something is too tight somewhere.

• The headpiece and browband should not be so tight that they pull towards the base of the ears and press into them, rub or actually damage the skin.

• The headpiece should lie at least 1 cm (½ in) behind the base of the ears. If it doesn't, the browband is probably too short and pulling the headpiece forwards and/or the headpiece is too wide.

• Conversely, the browband should not be so loose that it flops about.

• The throatlatch should be loose enough to fall halfway down the horse's round jawbones. You should be able to fit the width of your hand comfortably sideways between the bone and the strap.

Fitting a curb chain

A curb chain should lie well down in the chin groove, not riding up the lower jawbones, which are only thinly covered by skin. You should be able to slide one finger along under the chain. The chain should come into action when the lower cheek of the curb bit is drawn back to a 45-degree angle with the line of the horse's lips. If it is tighter than this, it can create too fixed a feel in the horse's mouth. If it is looser, the rider needs to pull to get any reaction at all and the bit will not be acting correctly.

• The cheekpieces and the straps to which the noseband is attached should lie well back from the eyes so as not to rub them. Often, the part of the noseband around the jawbones is too short or fitted too tightly, which pulls the vertical strap forward.

• A noseband that encircles the top and lower jaws should lie about midway between the corners of the lips and the sharp facial bones.

Fitting a bit

With any bit, you should be able to fit the width of one finger between the bit ring or cheek (not the bridle cheekpiece) and the horse's cheek. Bits currently come in increments of 13 mm ($\frac{1}{2}$ in). Measure your horse's present bit along the mouthpiece inside the rings or cheeks. Then, using the guideline above, decide whether you need a larger or smaller size.

• A bit with a jointed mouthpiece should normally be adjusted so that it makes just *one* wrinkle of skin at the corners of the horse's mouth.

• A mullen-mouthed snaffle, pelham, kimblewick or Western curb (all non-jointed mouthpieces) should fit snugly up against the corners of the mouth *without creating any wrinkles at all*.

• A curb bit used as part of a double bridle should lie about 1 cm ($\frac{1}{2}$ in) below the bridoon. It must not touch the corners of the lips at all. The bridoon lies on top of it.

A horse needs to be comfortable in order to do his best work. Fitting the bridle comfortably, as here, goes a long way towards helping your horse.

Reins

Reins are available in various lengths, but many of those sold today are too short. Showjumping reins may be fairly short because of the slightly forward jumping seat. Others should allow the rider to sit upright in the saddle with elbows well back at the hips while allowing the horse to put his muzzle on the ground with no rein contact.

Reins that are too short hamper correct flatwork by giving the horse the feeling that he cannot get his head down to stretch. They also encourage the rider to ride with their hands too far forward and arms straight, which does not make for a sensitive feel.

Beware of fashion

Think very carefully about your horse's comfort in his bridle and don't just follow fashion. The modern fashion is to fit bits too high in the mouth and to fasten nosebands too tightly. It does not take much imagination to realize how very uncomfortable, probably painful and certainly counter-productive this is, because no one can get the best from an unhappy, uncomfortable, distressed horse.

High bits

The reasoning behind adjusting bits so high that they create two or even more wrinkles at the corners of the mouth is that this makes the horse more sensitive to the bit contact. In fact, the reverse is true. Stretched skin is painful and can split, which is very bad horsemastership. It also allows the rider no finesse at all in giving the aids, and if the skin splits a callous often forms, making the lips quite insensitive.

Tight nosebands

The idea behind tight nosebands is to prevent or discourage the horse from opening his mouth and/or crossing his jaw, thereby evading the action of the bit. The aim of all good horsemen is for their horse to be able to flex or 'give' to the bit and mouth it gently. To do this the horse must move his jaws, and to move his jaws he must open his mouth very slightly by dropping his bottom jaw. He cannot do this if it is strapped shut. Therefore, by shutting the mouth the rider is actually preventing the horse doing what they are asking him to do.

Putting on a bridle

Horses are normally very protective of their heads, so it is no wonder that some become headshy through experiencing discomfort when having their bridles put on and taken off. Trying to put on a bridle that does not fit will be uncomfortable and may cause the horse to resist, so check beforehand that it probably fits well by holding it up against the side of the horse's head and seeing where the headpiece and bit lie.

Checklist
- ✓ bridling procedure
- ✓ be considerate throughout
- ✓ take care when unbridling
- ✓ bridling outside safely
- ✓ bitless bridles

Bridling

Before putting on the bridle, make sure the throatlatch and noseband (and curb chain, if applicable) are undone. Place the reins over the horse's head with the buckle just behind the ears so that, should he move away, you can catch hold of them under his throat and keep control of his head.

Standing on the left side of the horse's head with your back to his tail, hold the headpiece with your right hand and with your left ease the bit into the horse's mouth by putting your thumb into his mouth at the side where there are no teeth. Most horses open up quickly and you can slip the bit in.

Now lift up the bridle and ease the headpiece gently over first one ear and then the other. Straighten out the hair under the headpiece so that it is comfortable and pull out the forelock so that it hangs over the browband. See that the bridle is straight on the horse's head and the bit even (level) on both sides. Check that the browband sits just below the ears and is level because if it isn't, or it pulls at the headpiece, the horse will be uncomfortable. Fasten the throatlatch – and now you can put the buckle of the reins back on to the horse's withers.

The noseband straps should lie underneath the bridle cheekpieces. Fasten the noseband and adjust it according to its type. Remember, you must be able to slide a finger easily all around under all the straps when they are done up.

If your bridle has a curb chain, fasten it now. It will be hanging on the right hook. Take it in your right hand and twist it clockwise to make sure all the metal links are flat and smooth. Hook the last link on the left hook and adjust the length by slotting other links on to the hooks. Make sure the chain is flat and not twisted.

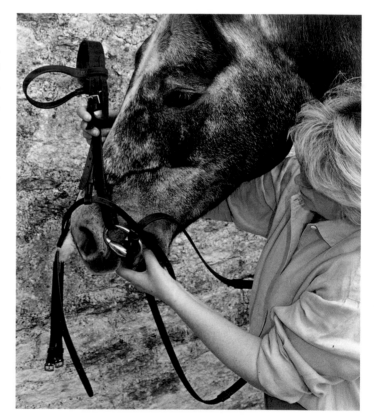

1 *Talk to your horse quietly and confidently while you are putting on his bridle. Many people like to give a titbit beforehand, not just for bribery (!) but to get the horse's mouth moving and leave him with a pleasant taste in his mouth. Be sure that you press the bit against where his top and bottom teeth meet to get him to open his mouth, and not on his gums by mistake, which can hurt.*

DO

- Talk to the horse as you approach him with the bridle (and saddle).
- Be gentle when bridling, and take your time.
- Check that all your tack is secure before mounting.

DON'T

- Rush any stages of the bridling (and saddling) process.
- Bang the bit against the horse's teeth.
- Try to mount until you have checked that all your tack is secure – and the girth is tight enough.

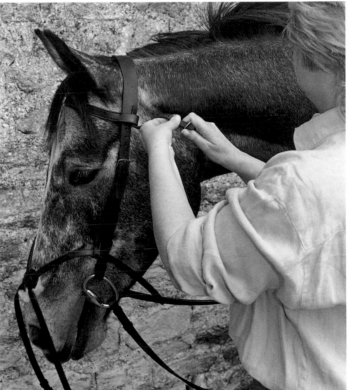

2 *Be confident when lifting up the headpiece. If you dawdle the horse will let go of the bit and you will have to start again. However, don't rush the horse: hold up the bridle properly and put the headpiece carefully over his ears.*

3 *It is correct to fasten the throatlatch first, then the noseband and finally, if appropriate, the curb chain. Conversely, unfasten from bottom to top (curb chain, noseband and throatlatch). This is said to make for security by keeping the throatlatch fastened for as long as possible. However, in some very respected schools of thought the bridle does not even have a throatlatch!*

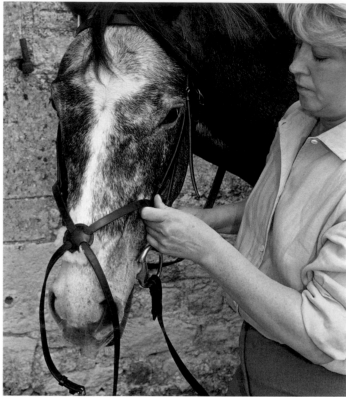

4 After all the straps are fastened, make sure that nothing is too tight (a major fault today) by running a finger all the way around the bridle under every strap, including over the nose. If you cannot do this, something is too tight somewhere and the horse will be uncomfortable. A tight bridle, contrary to popular opinion, does not make for more control but makes the horse very uncomfortable and, in some cases, likely to fight the discomfort.

5 The throatlatch on this bridle should be two or three holes looser. A throatlatch that the horse can feel pressing into his throat discourages him from flexing softly to the bit, something we always aim for in good riding.

Leading a horse in a bridle

To lead a horse in a bridle, bring the reins over his head and hold them together, using them like a leadrope.

Putting on a bridle outside

1 Have the horse tied up or hold him in a headcollar. Undo the headstrap of the headcollar and drop the noseband down over the nose, then do up the headstrap again so that it secures him around the top of his neck.

2 Put on the bridle as described above, then undo the headstrap of the headcollar to release it.

3 Do not leave the headcollar hanging down against the wall in case the horse gets a foot caught in it.

Unbridling

1 Undo the curb chain, noseband and throatlatch, in that order.

2 Bring the buckle of the reins up to the headpiece and, standing in front and slightly to one side of the horse's head, ease the reins and the headpiece carefully forward over his ears. Most horses are happy to drop their heads for this.

3 Do not under any circumstances pull the bit out of the horse's mouth. As you bring the headpiece forward over the ears, most horses will let go of the bit. If yours doesn't, wait for him to open his mouth. Keep the headpiece up level with the base of his ears so that it, not his teeth, takes the weight of the bit when he lets it go. Then slowly let it come down – and praise the horse.

Bitless bridles

Bitless bridles have always been used and have enjoyed varying levels of popularity. There are several different types.

Although we should always aim to control and communicate with our horse more with our seat and legs than with our hands via the reins to the bit, the majority of riders feel safer with a bit in their horse's mouth. Bitless bridles are not allowed in formal dressage competitions because one of the gauges of a horse's schooling (training) in this discipline is how well he accepts the bit. Others feel that it demonstrates the ultimate in the horse/rider bond if the horse can be trusted not only without a bit but also in some cases without even a bridle.

Some horses, having been abused in the mouth by harsh riding in the past, are never happy with a bit in their mouths and some have mouths of awkward conformation, which makes it difficult to find a bit to suit them. Also, if a horse has a sore mouth for any reason, a bitless bridle means he can continue to be worked and exercised while it heals.

Some bitless bridles are very strong in their action while others are extremely mild. The Western hackamore bridle works on the principle of a plaited, stiffened leather, oval-shaped nose piece called a bosal, which is finely balanced on the nose and has rope reins fastened to it under the horse's lower jaw. When the rider lifts his or her hands, the bosal tips down on to the nose, communicating by pressure there. This hackamore is used in the early training of Western horses.

Another very mild bitless bridle is the side-pull. This is simply a noseband around the horse's head above the nostrils, with reins fixed on left and right, which the rider pulls on or vibrates, one at a time for turns or both at once to slow down or stop.

A similar bridle is the Scawbrig, but here the front part of the noseband is padded and has rings at each end. Through these rings a continuous rein is threaded, passing under the horse's lower jaw and fastening by a buckle at the end held by the rider. Usually, the piece behind the horse's chin is widened and padded for comfort and to stop it sliding right through the rings. If the rider pulls on this continuous rein, there is a tightening effect around the horse's upper and lower jaws, which gives some direction and control.

One of the strongest bitless bridles that operates on a leverage system and which can actually fracture a horse's nose bone if harshly used, is the Blair, often incorrectly called a hackamore. There is a noseband around the upper and lower jaws, as usual, but from its sides drop two metal cheeks of varying lengths according to the rider's preference. The reins are fastened to the bottom rings of these cheeks and, when pulled, they tighten a strap behind the lower jaw and also tighten the front nose piece, as well as, in some types, causing a downward pressure, via the bridle cheekpieces, on the horse's poll, so the head can experience a vice-like gripping feel. Needless to say, such bridles should be used only by sensitive, knowledgeable riders with a truly independent seat in the saddle, so that there is no danger of their using the reins harshly to keep their balance.

Using a neckstrap

A neckstrap is useful for the rider to hold on to for security, if necessary. It consists simply of a strap, such as an old stirrup leather, that is fastened around the horse's neck.

Boots and bandages

Horses' legs are only very thinly protected by skin. The bones, tendons and ligaments are therefore extremely vulnerable, not only to strains and sprains but also to knocks, treads and general injuries. Many people turn their horses out in boots and, for short periods, this is an excellent idea. There are boots and bandaging systems for support, holding on dressings, protection, travelling, drying the legs and warmth.

Checklist
✓ boot types and styles
✓ exercise and stable bandages
✓ putting on and removing safely

Protective boots

If your horse is inclined to kick himself (called 'interfering' or 'brushing'), or if he is jumped or lunged, he will need protective boots for his legs.

Brushing boots Use a design with reinforced pads or shields that fit down the inner side of the leg and fetlock for forelegs or hindlegs, hindleg boots always being slightly longer than foreleg boots of any kind. Horses that interfere high up the leg are said to 'speedicut' and you can buy longer boots for this problem.

Shin boots These have padding down the front of the cannon (shin) bones to protect jumping horses from hurting themselves on poles, and some incorporate brushing shields as well.

Tendon boots These do not actually prevent strain and sprain of tendons, but are intended to protect the forelegs from the horse hitting into them from behind with the toes of his hind feet. They have padding down the back of the leg and reinforced but flexible bars inside the boot that fit down the sides of the tendons for stability.

There are also boots that are scientifically proven to help reduce the concussion and strain on the tendons and ligaments of performance horses, and those under particular stress may well benefit. Different names are given to them by their manufacturers. Some of them can be tricky to put on but a little practise will soon make you proficient.

Over-reach or bell boots These are bell-shaped boots made from rubber or synthetic material, which protect a horse's heels and the sides of the coronets from self-inflicted treads. They are normally worn on the forelegs, but bell boots all round when travelling offer good protection to all four feet.

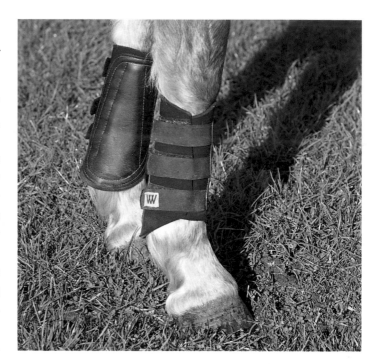

These are synthetic brushing boots for the forelegs. They have reinforced shields down the insides and fasten on the outsides.

Putting on and taking off boots

1 Place the boot in the appropriate place on the leg and fasten it from the bottom up. If you fasten it from the top down, should the horse move during the process it may slide down, flop over the hoof and trip the horse.
2 For the same reason, when taking boots off undo them from the top down.
3 Once the boots have been removed, give the legs a brisk rub to stimulate the skin.

A word of warning

It is known that boots and bandages encourage the central core of the tendons to heat up, and in this state they are more prone to injury. Some experts – both scientists and professional horsemen – believe that regularly working horses in boots, particularly support boots, denies the legs the chance to strengthen and toughen naturally. A good compromise seems to be to use boots only for fast work, jumping and competition, and to remove them as soon as possible afterwards.

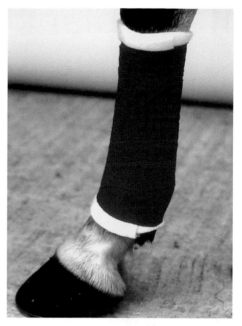

This well-applied exercise or work bandage has been placed over felt padding and the pressure appears even. The end of the bandage is pointing backwards and the tapes have been tucked under a layer of bandage.

Travelling boots These cover the whole lower leg with padding, from above the knee or hock right down to the ground in some cases. They are quick and easy to put on, and protect your horse's legs while he is travelling in the trailer or horsebox.

Fastening systems in most boots consist of Velcro straps, sometimes assisted by clips and hooks of various kind – the latter are certainly advisable for work boots.

Bandages

Apart from veterinary bandages, there are two sorts of bandage (wrap).

Exercise bandages These are normally made of stretchy crêpe and are put on over padding to protect the skin and to guard against possible uneven pressure during application, which can be extremely damaging to the legs. Proprietary paddings such as synthetic felts can be used, or the traditional gamgee tissue – cottonwool covered with gauze.

Unless the bandages interfere with the action of the fetlock joint (which they should not), they cannot support the leg but may possibly reduce concussion and vibration in the leg caused by work.

Stable bandages are longer and wider than exercise bandages, the most useful sort being made from knitted material, which moulds to the leg. Again, they are put on over padding and are used to dry off legs, provide warmth, comfort and/or support, and to keep dressings in place.

Putting on and taking off bandages

Exercise bandages are put on from just below the knee or hock to just above the fetlock joint, although if extended under the joint at the back they may provide slight support for the tendons and ligaments. It is essential to apply exercise bandages firmly but not tightly and with even pressure.

• On the near-side (left) legs, apply the bandages in an anti-clockwise direction, winding down and back up the leg, and try to finish with the end carrying the fastening pointing backwards on the outside of the leg. This is so that it cannot so easily pick up twigs and debris during work or be hit by the horse's opposing leg.

• On the off-side (right) legs, apply bandages clockwise for the same reason.

Stable bandages are applied in a similar way to exercise bandages, but are taken all the way down the leg to the coronet and back up again.

• Apply stable bandages more loosely than exercise bandages, especially if you are using them for injured, swollen legs – just tightly enough to keep them on.

• To remove bandages, undo the fastenings and quickly pass the bandage from hand to hand around the leg, making no attempt to roll it up as you do so. Rub the legs briskly unless they are injured. Roll up the bandage afterwards, away from the horse.

Rugs, blankets and sheets

There is a vast array of different kinds of horse clothing available. Some items may be useful, but very many horses, and even ponies, today are overloaded with clothing they do not need, which makes them very uncomfortable and which they would be happier without. Clothing should be used to help the horse only when really necessary, and not used simply because the owner feels that she is 'looking after' her horse.

Checklist
✓ rugs for indoors
✓ exercise sheets
✓ rugs for outdoors
✓ fitting rugs
✓ is your horse cold or hot?

Water- and windproof rugs are a boon to a horse out for long periods in wet and windy weather. This rug fits well at the back but should come further forward.

during the variable temperatures of spring and autumn, so that you use the correct amount and weight of clothing on your horse.

Exercise clothing

Most horses do not need exercise or 'quarter' sheets, but thin-coated, fine-skinned and clipped horses in winter – particularly those with the hair removed from the back, loins and hindquarters – may well benefit mentally and physically from an exercise sheet, which may be waterproof. Cold muscles are more easily strained and injured than warm ones, and a sheet can certainly help.

There are various patterns available, from light rain sheets to wonderful, warm woollen ones. The idea is that the sheet should extend from the withers right to the root of the tail. Some stop at the croup, but these leave exposed the very muscles that need protecting. Use a sheet that is the right length to do the job properly – and always use a fillet string under the tail to prevent the sheet blowing up and terrifying the horse.

High-visibility sheets should be used for horses in traffic, maybe over another type, as required.

Stable clothing

Clothing for the horse to wear in his stable varies from lightweight summer dust sheets to padded, duvet-like winter 'cover-alls'. Textiles vary, too, but most rugs these days are made from permeable fabrics that protect the horse but allow natural body sweat to evaporate through the fabric – provided the horse is not overloaded with rugs.

In summer, a very light sheet can protect a stabled horse from dust and there are special mesh ones to protect against insects. Winter clothing comes in various weights and the correct weight to use is the lightest that will keep the horse comfortably warm – *not* hot. Extra vigilance is needed

Turnout clothing

Turnout clothing for summer usually comprises mesh sheets to guard against insects, which generally cover the neck and belly as well as the body, and those designed to protect the coat from bleaching by the sun.

There are lightweight, lined sheets for chilly spring and autumn weather, and some winter rugs that are almost like portable, padded tents! A really well-fitting, padded, water- and windproof rug or two can be a real boon for horses in winter (as can mud chaps for the legs, which really seem to help protect against infections such as mud fever). Neck covers and tail flaps can be a comfort to horses who feel the cold, and pleats and darts should be incorporated at elbow and stifle to ensure there is room to move. Modern patterns are well designed to accommodate the undulating shape of a horse's body, which helps to keep the rug in place.

Be prepared

Your horse should really have two of any kind of rug, blanket or sheet, so that they can all be kept decently clean and, if necessary, repaired. Because clothing can be expensive, many owners have a main rug and a cheaper alternative for short periods while the main one is drying or being mended. This is particularly important with anti-midge sheets in summer, and warm clothing in winter.

Correct fit

The main problems with most rugs come at the front end, because rugs nearly always slide backwards with the hair. Rubbed and bald shoulders are still far too common as are pressured withers, and rugs with necklines that nearly choke the horse when he tries to get his head down.

Look for modern design features, such as V-shaped front fastenings, which take the pressure off the points of the shoulders and keep the rug forward, without pressing on the horse's neck underneath or the withers on top.

A basic rug should extend forward with the neckline in front of the withers, never on top of or behind them, and reach the root of the tail behind (a little longer in turnout rugs). In depth, they should reach down to elbow and stifle for indoor rugs, longer where extra warmth is required and for turnout rugs.

The old way of securing rugs was with a roller. Modern rugs have leg straps and/or surcingles (straps) crossing under the belly.

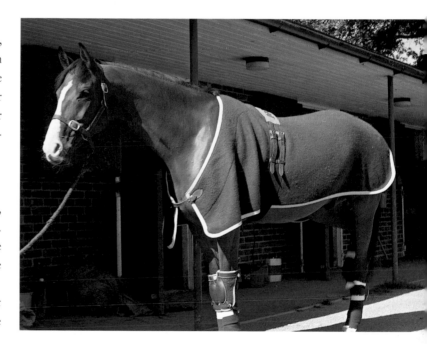

There are several ways to tell if a horse is cold or hot

• Place your hand around the base of his ears. If they are cold, so is the horse.

• Place the flat of your hand on his belly, loins, flanks and rump and allow a few seconds for the skin temperature to register. If he feels genuinely cool, he could do with one mediumweight rug; if he is actually cold, a warmer rug can be used.

• Horses shiver like us when they are really cold, so watch out for this.

• A really cold horse may be hunched up and/or his hair may be standing on end.

• If your horse is clearly very warm to the touch and damp from sweat, whether he has been working or not, he is obviously too hot and needs cooling down, not rugging up.

• Remove any clothing and try to put him in an airflow, natural or fan-generated.

• If he is seriously hot, sponge or hose him down with cool water, then leave him to stand (because movement creates heat) and evaporate away the heat.

• A traditional mesh anti-sweat rug can create cooling eddies of air over the skin when hot horses are walked in the shade.

• American all-over coolers are not suitable for this purpose, but are fine for drying off hot horses on cool days.

Rugging up

Always approach an unknown horse carefully and place the rug over his saddle area first to see how he reacts, then proceed from there. Youngsters should be allowed to get used to the sight and smell of rugs. Lay them over the stable door or manger, stay with the horse and don't make a fuss. Let him take his time investigating them and have someone else present when you rug him up for the first time.

Checklist

✓ safe rugging-up procedures
✓ comfort is paramount
✓ safe off-rugging

Putting on a rug

Rugging up properly will ensure that your horse feels comfortable and that the rug cannot slip around and trip him up.

Method 1

1 Check that there are no bits of bedding on the inside (lining) of the rug, which will irritate the horse when it is on. Take the rug with one hand at each end of the seam that runs along the horse's backbone (or where the seam would be if the rug does not have one) and place it, bunched together, over the withers.

2 Pull the back edge of the rug back in the direction of the hair, so that it comes just in front of the root of the tail and the seam runs directly along the horse's spine.

3 Fasten the surcingles and/or leg straps first, so that if the horse moves and the rug slips it will fall backwards and slide off over his hindquarters, where he can step out of it. If you fasten the front (breast) straps first, the rug will be firmly fastened around his neck and will slide around, remaining fixed and trailing on the floor where the horse could tread on it and bring himself down.

4 Sort out the front comfortably and fasten the breast straps. Smooth down the mane hair under the front of the rug to its natural side. Do not pull the rug further back. The problem with rugs is keeping them forward, although well-fitting rugs stay in place reasonably well, so pulling a rug back will just tighten it up around the shoulders and make the horse uncomfortable.

DO

• Lay or hang your rug, lining outwards, to air every day. Horse rugs soon become damp from sweat and need to dry off, otherwise they become heavy, smelly and unhygienic.

• Keep your rugs in good repair, for safety and economy.

• Keep your rugs reasonably clean. Many can be washed in a domestic washing machine and there are specialist equine laundries in many areas. Try to wash your rugs weekly. (See also pages 102–103.)

DON'T

• Let rug linings pick up debris and bits of bedding, which can really irritate the horse's skin.

• Put on any more rugs than strictly necessary for your horse's comfort. Overloading causes overheating and makes your horse miserable and uncomfortable – not a way to show that you care.

• Swap rugs between horses without washing them, to prevent the possible spread of disease.

Method 2

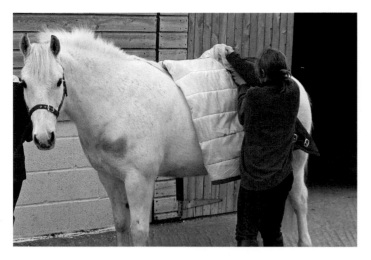

1 *Fold the rug in half across its width with the lining exposed, then lay it well forward over the horse's loins.*

2 *Bring the front half forward to well in front of the withers and move it back only slightly to smooth out the hair, so that it remains around the bottom of the neck – not back on the withers and down on the shoulders.*

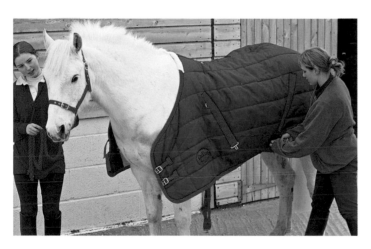

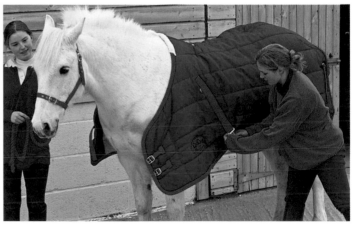

3 *Fasten the leg straps first...*

4 *then the surcingles (most rugs don't have both)...*

5 *and finally the breast straps.*

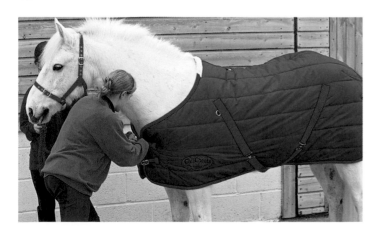

You should be able to fit the width of your hand sideways between the surcingles and the horse's belly and the same with the leg straps, if any. You should also be able to slide your hand easily all round the neckline.

Care of rugs and blankets

Good-quality horse clothing is expensive and it makes good sense to make it last as long as possible by looking after it. Get repairs done quickly and help fabrics last longer by keeping them clean, using the right products. Many owners are content to keep their horses in damp, filthy, smelly rugs, which indicates very low horse-care standards. Make sure that you would be happy to wrap your horse's rug around yourself!

Checklist
✓ look after your rugs
✓ where to hang rugs
✓ cleaning rugs
✓ storage
✓ natural versus synthetic

Take care

Cultivate the same sort of protective attitude towards your rugs as you do your tack. Many people take great care of their tack, whether leather or synthetic, but treat horse clothing as if it were disposable or not important. Regarding it as something precious and important, not to mention expensive (which it is), instils an attitude of protection and care, which will help it to last longer.

Daily use

Be careful where you put your rugs. Put them down in a clean, dry place – don't just dump them on the horse's bedding or the ground. Leaving rugs lying around on abrasive, gritty surfaces such as concrete, sand or earth wears the fabric fibres and spoils the finish. Grit gets into the fabric, wears it away and irritates your horse, as do bits of hay and bedding.

When rugs are not in use, the ideal place for them is hanging – lining outwards to air – on a special rack or even just over a fence or hedge. They should certainly be aired every day, if at all possible. Do not leave them below birds'

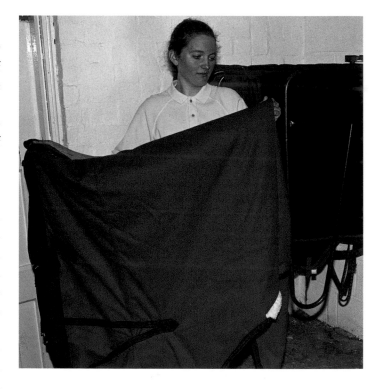

Rugs can be kept in good condition by being hung on proper rug racks in the tack room – heated models help with drying and airing.

How many rugs?

Ideally, you should have three of every type of rug you need, but this may not be possible. The old advice was always: one on, one ready and one in the wash. Certainly, you need two of whatever rugs you use regularly (see pages 98–99).

nests or roosts, however, as they will become soiled by bird droppings. While you are out riding is the ideal time to air your rugs.

If this is not possible, fold the rug, lining in, and hang it over the stable door, lay it on the manger or, if necessary, in a clean corner of the stable. Shake out the rug before replacing it on your horse.

Laundering or cleaning

The golden rule is to follow the manufacturer's instructions. Most synthetic rugs can be washed at home in a very mild detergent, with fabric softener in the final rinse. Thicker rugs can be washed at a launderette, or washed or dry cleaned by a specialist equine laundry. Make sure that you point out the manufacturer's instructions to them. If not stitched to the rug, pin them on yourself so that there can be no misunderstanding. You don't want your rugs ruined.

Short-term storage

Rugs can be laundered or dry cleaned and, if not required for a few days or weeks, hung on a rug rack, of which there are several designs available. Alternatively, store your rugs in a cupboard, chest or drawers.

Long-term storage

Make sure rugs are clean, and preferably repaired, before they are put away for the season. This is good for the fabric and ensures that they are ready in good condition when needed again. Over a long period, dirty rugs, even synthetic ones, attract insects and rodents to nest and breed in them. Natural fibres can also be eaten by moths.

Most horse clothing is synthetic these days, but if yours has leather parts ensure that these are very well oiled before storage to keep them supple and free from cracks. Clean the buckles so that they are free from rust and verdigris, which can damage leather.

Synthetic or natural fibres?

Most rugs today are synthetic, but natural fibres do have a lot going for them and are still available. For instance, there is nothing quite like a woollen exercise/quarter sheet on a cold, windy, drizzly day. It will keep a sensitive horse warm and dry, drape comfortably around him and protect him like nothing else can.

Synthetics, of course, have the advantage of being very easily washed and dried, and are light and warm. They come into their own as turnout rugs: because they are easy to keep clean (unlike traditional proofed canvas), you can always have a dry, clean rug ready for your horse's turnout time. The choice is yours.

The best place to store clothing is in a clean, dry trunk or a chest of drawers. If you are a livery owner and there is nowhere suitable to keep your rugs at your yard, take them home until needed, where they can be stored safely in clean, dry conditions.

From left to right: A lightweight cotton summer sheet, a synthetic multi-purpose rug and a woollen winter day or travelling rug.

Yard or barn equipment

They say that a poor workman always blames his tools, but the right tools and equipment make work so much easier and generally improve the result. Horse chores are labour intensive and anything you can do, within reason, to cut down on the work while not compromising on your horse's care must be worthwhile. Whether you spend out on mechanical aids or simply buy top-quality manual gear, it's money well spent.

Checklist
✓ avoid false economies
✓ choose the right equipment for you
✓ make the most of mechanization
✓ choose well-designed equipment
✓ put the horse before yard chores

Small, single-wheeled barrows make mucking out a real chore! They are only really suitable for skipping out droppings.

push and balance at the same time. In addition, they do not tip over, dropping muck on the yard.

If you have two or more horses, it's worth getting a large, four-wheeled barrow, perhaps with a hydraulic or other type of system that, at the push of a lever, lifts the body of the barrow, depositing the muck on the muck heap for you. You'll be blessing it years after you've forgotten how much it cost.

Brooms

Sweeping the yard is another time-consuming chore that can be greatly reduced by buying a wide-headed yard-sweeping broom, so that you sweep at least twice as much yard with one push as with a normal brush. Always buy natural fibre brooms: these last longer and do the job better. Synthetic ones 'fray' and split, quickly accumulating bedding and debris amongst the bristles.

Barrows

The yard equipment you will use most often is mucking-out gear. The most common mistake here is to get a tiny wheelbarrow with only one central wheel, because it is cheap. This is definitely false economy.

A small barrow will necessitate several trips to the muck heap, where one would do with a larger two-wheeled barrow. Two-wheeled barrows with a central axle are very easy to push and balance, and you don't need to lift them,

Skips

Most people now use plastic mesh laundry baskets as muck skips and they are ideal. Tough rubber or synthetic gloves and a basket make skipping out easy – unless you have back problems, in which case you need a muck scoop and strong rake so that you can rake the droppings into the scoop and then tip them into the basket. The scoop and rake also work very well when picking up droppings from paddocks and turnout areas.

Shovels

Wide-blade shovels are much more use than the normal kind, although it is handy to have a few of both types. Plastic blades break easily and wear badly.

Forks

Four-tined forks are universally useful in yards for use with bedding of any kind. Shavings rakes are of limited value: they simply mix the clean bedding in with the damp and their short prongs are relatively ineffective. Close-tined forks are good for removing droppings from any bed but long straw.

Motorized help

If you have the cash and the need, motorized vacuum 'poo-picking' machines are ideal for keeping paddocks clean. The ride-on type are ideal for the elderly – or the lazy!

These vacuum machines are also excellent to save time on the chore of sweeping the yard. Anyone can use them, and for larger yards they are worth the investment. Such machines need regular servicing.

Get your priorities right

Yard chores can very easily take over from the more important tasks of actually looking after your horse. The horses are the entire reason for the existence of the yard, and their needs should always come before such tasks as sweeping or vacuuming the yard, tidying the muck heap, cleaning windows, tending garden areas, clearing out the tack room and so on. Time-saving equipment is an excellent investment, as it frees you to be with your horse.

Paid help

The advantage of well-designed equipment, manual or motorized, is that it makes chores easier. Because of this, it also makes it easier to get non-specialized, paid help to do the yard jobs. No equestrian knowledge is required to sweep a yard, poo-pick a paddock (manually or by machine) or even muck out.

A neat and tidy yard creates a good impression but the happiness of the horses is more important. Don't get carried away with your chores to the point where you are short of time for your horse.

Transporting horses

Many people who are seriously interested in 'going places' with their horse have their own transport. This brings its own problems. Many otherwise well-behaved horses take great exception to being loaded up, travelling and even unloading. If introduced properly and carried out well, these should not create hassle. There are certain common-sense pros and cons to take into account when transporting horses.

Some horses need a little time to be sure that the inside of the box is safe, but others plant themselves on the ramp and refuse to move.

Equine fact

Research and observation has shown that black-coloured matting on ramps and inside vehicles greatly worries some horses, to the point where they will not load. Green has been found to be much less frightening, as is red.

Your horse's attitude

Some horses have been frightened, angered or completely misunderstood when attempts have been made to load them in the past. This 'baggage' comes with them to a new home and many amateur owners are clueless as to how to cope. With some horses, it only takes one bad experience to make them bad to load. Others can have the most appalling accidents and then load and travel perfectly afterwards as if nothing ever happened.

Your attitude

The most common mistake is to believe that the horse thinks like a human. He does not. The human has to learn to think like a horse if loading and travelling are to be a successful venture.

You need to understand that the inside of a trailer is most unappealing to a horse standing outside it, particularly if it is dark, small and there is no escape route at the other end. In most countries, too, the trailers or floats available accommodate horses standing 'head to the engine', yet it is quite widely acknowledged that horses generally travel far better 'tail to the engine', and often herringbone-style with their quarters towards the driver and their heads towards the kerb. Horses balance better this way and so travel better and are less likely to associate transport vehicles with fear and distress.

Let the horse teach himself

One virtually sure-fire way to get a horse to load trouble-free is to leave the trailer or horsebox in his paddock with the ramp down, ideally up a slope to reduce its angle, with

Here the horse is investigating the inside of the vehicle and his handler, with a long lead for safety and security, is encouraging him.

the entrance facing the sun. Particularly if there is a front ramp down as well, a horse's curiosity will eventually get the better of him and usually, after a time, he will load himself and walk out the other way, and vice versa. Where 'problem loaders' are concerned, by all means leave tasty treats and feed in the vehicle and stay out of the way. A few days or weeks of this has transformed many horses for life.

Trailer or horsebox?

There can be no doubt that a horsebox is preferable to a trailer, but the added expense cannot be justified by most owners. Trailers will continue to be more popular for this reason alone, however the advantages of a horsebox include the following:

• The 'ride' given by a decent, even small horsebox is far superior to that of a trailer.
• There is no risk of jack-knifing.
• You do not need to hitch up and unhitch.
• Stability is greater during adverse weather conditions.
• Horseboxes can fairly easily be converted so that the horses can travel facing backwards. With a trailer, this would involve moving the axle so that the horse, with his heavier forehand facing to the rear, would not tip the trailer up off its hitch. Rear-facing trailers are available in some

A free hand

When permitted, horses travel much better not tied up and given the whole horsebox to travel in. This is the standard way to travel a mare and foal. However, horses travelled free in trailers may turn round and dangerously upset the trailer's balance.

countries but you have to search them out.
The disadvantages of a horsebox include the following:
• More expense in the form of road tax and insurance.
• Increased maintenance and servicing charges.

On the road

The most important thing to remember here is to *drive as though you had no brakes*.

It is the variations in speed, balance and tilt during acceleration, braking and cornering, even moving from lane to lane, that upset the precarious balance of most horses travelling facing forwards. If the driver maintains as constant a speed and direction as possible in transit, the horse's problems will be greatly reduced.

Horses should wear protective gear on a journey and a reinforced poll guard to protect the head would also be beneficial.

RIDING

There is nothing quite like the thrill of riding a horse. This is why most people associate with them – although some never ride, just wanting to be with them and look after them. It is an unexpected relationship, when a prey animal allows a predator to sit on him, never mind being willing to do peculiar things the horse would never normally do, in partnership with the predator. This shows how adaptable horses are, and how amenable when treated properly. It is sad when some humans abuse this trust by not trying to ride well.

Clothing

Riding clothing was designed for comfort, practicality and safety. There are informal and formal outfits, varying with the sport involved. For everyday riding, you just need to be comfortable, safe, cool in summer and warm in winter. A cold body does not work well and you need all your faculties to be able to ride optimally and cope in an emergency, such as if the horse becomes frightened.

Checklist
✓ safety first
✓ be comfortable
✓ essential clothing
✓ where to buy

Safety and comfort

Top of the list must always come safety – so make sure that what you wear is safe for the job, practical and, of course, comfortable. Some people put themselves through unnecessary agony by failing to appreciate how much friction there may be on their legs when riding, so it is most important to ensure you have thick trousers or jodhpurs, or use some undergear to prevent blisters and rubs until your skin becomes toughened. Gloves are important as they protect your hands.

Basic clothing

Different types of riding may merit different kit, but the essentials to get started are given below.

Hat You will need a hard hat with a secure fastening. Before buying, check that the hat is an approved design and conforms to the safety standards of your country. A hat must be the right size and fit snugly, and must be secured tightly enough to keep it on at all times when mounted. It is not clever to ride without head protection or to refuse to fasten your hat securely enough. These may be insurance requirements anyway.

Boots Short boots with a low heel, or long leather or rubber riding boots are ideal. They must fit closely to your leg and have a relatively smooth sole so that they do not stick in the stirrups. Half chaps used with short jodhpur boots are also popular. These are individual leg protectors that fit from below the knee to the foot, as opposed to full chaps, which cover the whole leg and fasten around the waist.

Jodhpurs These are specifically designed for riders and have knee padding positioned to prevent friction rubs. Breeches

Western style

Western riders usually wear a stetson hat, which in its basic form offers no protection, although there are newer designs with protection built in. Cowboy-style boots with a higher heel are traditional, but not essential to start with. When Western riders wear jeans they usually wear leather or suede full chaps on top for extra protection; these also give a more stable feel to the leg.

(a shorter-legged version) are good for use with long boots or half chaps. Tough jeans or trousers can be used if you are just starting to ride at walk, but are not recommended for serious riding.

Gloves Those made from string or fabric – especially with a rubber or synthetic pimple insert on the palm – give good grip and will protect your hands from blisters or sores caused by rubs from the reins.

Body protector This is a wise investment, especially when you progress to serious riding and jumping. Buy one that is comfortable to wear but also protective. Choose a protector recommended by your riding school, teacher or consultant, and of an approved safety design. Many riding schools supply body protectors for use on loan, along with hats and boots.

Shirt and jacket For your top half, it is normally advisable to wear long sleeves even in warm weather to protect against grazes should you fall.

• In hot weather, cotton shirts look the part and are very comfortable.

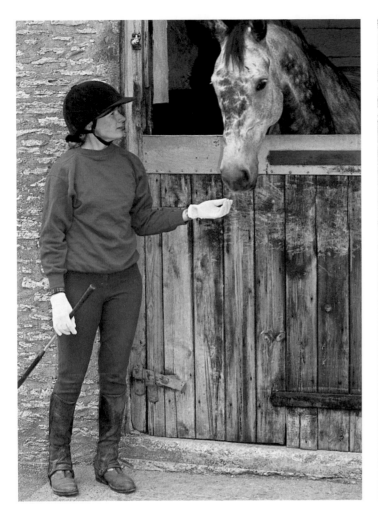

An informal, everyday outfit comprising skullcap, riding jeans, half-chaps, boots and gloves. A whip should not be necessary for a beginner.

A formal outfit used for competition, comprising a dark jacket, white hunting tie, long boots with spurs, breeches, gloves and a skullcap.

• In-between weather demands something warmer, maybe a woollen sweater, fleece, polo shirt over a tee shirt and so on.

• Really cold weather brings out the padded 'duvet' jackets. There are also long and short waterproof riding coats for rain and sleet.

• In adverse weather, use a coat long enough to cover your bottom and legs or at least your thighs, usually with adjustable side or back slits to drape comfortably over the saddle and horse's back.

Buying riding gear

It is possible to find nearly everything you will need in your local tack shop. Mail order catalogues can also be a good source, but there is the problem of having to return items if they do not fit. If you want to take part in a specific type of competition, it is always worth checking what gear you need before investing in any special kit.

When buying riding clothes, remember that you need a bit of room to move, especially with coats, to allow you freedom to mount and dismount. Tight clothing of whatever kind is not recommended for any type of riding. It is also cold in winter and hot in summer, which is not good.

If you live in a cold climate, it is worth getting boots large enough to fit some really thick socks inside them: icy toes are no fun at all on an early-morning ride.

There is nothing more frustrating than suffering from sores or blisters, so do take care to ensure you are wearing adequate clothing, especially on the most vulnerable areas – your legs, knees, ankles and hands.

Finding a riding school

In some areas, good riding schools are scarce because of the prohibitive costs of insurance, business rates and other expenses, and the rigours of health and safety regulations. Good schools are essential to beginners to ensure that they begin correctly, as safely as possible and are taught by professionals on 'schoolmaster' horses who know their jobs. Such well-behaved, well-trained horses are invaluable for looking after novices.

Checklist
- ✓ sources of information
- ✓ choose the best school you can
- ✓ visiting
- ✓ what to look for
- ✓ asking questions
- ✓ learn about riding

Visit a school and chat to other clients to learn about the horses and check out the atmosphere and general running of the place.

Where to look

You may already know of somewhere through friends or have been recommended to a particular riding school by a professional such as a vet or farrier. Local saddlery stores and feed merchants also usually have suitable contacts. Your regional business telephone book will list local riding schools, too.

In some countries, riding schools have to be licensed and may also be approved by a professional body. You can contact these organizations and ask for a list of approved establishments in your area.

Remember: it is better to travel to a good, approved yard some distance away and be in good hands than to go to a more dubious establishment nearby. Some riding centres now organize day and weekend courses for riders of different abilities. At a good school, there is little danger of your being put on a horse that does not suit you or mixed in with riders of a higher standard than you, who will be doing things that might frighten you to death – for now.

Visiting the school

When you have the telephone number of one or two suitable establishments, ring them up, tell them about yourself and

Check your riding school

When visiting a prospective riding school, ask yourself the following questions:
• Did you receive a friendly welcome?
• Is the muck heap fairly neat and tidy? Often, this is a good indication of how the rest of the yard is run.
• Is there a safe area or school in which novices can learn?
• Is the riding school approved by a recognized riding organization?
• Are the horses suitable for beginners and novices?

what you want, and ask if you can visit to look around and meet the staff and horses. No decent yard will object to this. Make an appointment and do your best to keep it. Most yards are very busy, and if you turn up unannounced they may not have time to attend to you.

Know your riding school

It is important to get to know the venue at which you plan to start riding and exactly what goes on there, as this helps you to be more confident and relaxed when it comes to mounting and riding for the first time or after a long break. Fear of the unknown is a common reaction, so it is a good plan to avoid this, if possible, by visiting.

The stable yard or barn should have a feeling of efficiency about it, with helpful staff who look after you, their client. The general neatness and tidiness will often be an indication of its standards. The atmosphere at a riding stables can tell you a lot about how well it is run, so check whether the horses and staff seem happy and willing to do what is expected of them. Dirty, unhappy horses and rough, slovenly staff should put you off.

Safety first

Check that the riding school has a health and safety policy, and whether or not you will be covered adequately by either your own insurance or that held by the yard. Never be afraid to ask questions about these issues, so that you fully understand the implications should you have a fall or other accident. Afterwards is too late.

A good school will also run lessons in horse care and management, called 'stable management' – these are just as absorbing as riding.

Prepare yourself

Some mental preparation is necessary for success.
• If you have not already seen much riding at first hand, take the trouble to watch some lessons, both private and in a class.
• Talk to people who ride so that you can begin to understand what is involved. Most riders are more than happy to tell you about their own riding experiences.
• You can also learn more from books (like this one), videos, DVDs and the internet. It is worth learning about the different types of riding, to see what you might be interested in trying.

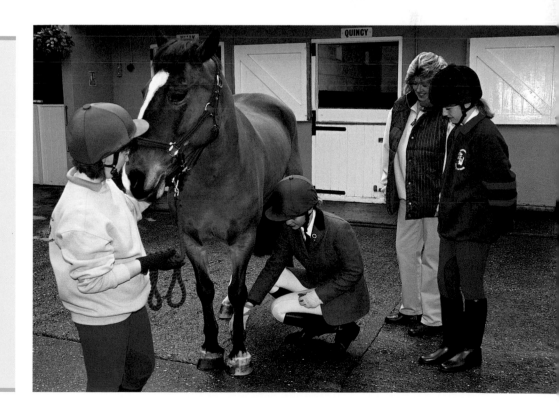

First lessons

You can book your first lesson over the telephone, but it is best to meet the staff and teachers. They will discuss procedures with you and introduce you to some of the horses and ponies. Do not be late as this may result in your not being able to ride. Most schools are busy and you may have to pay for a missed lesson. Arrive about half an hour early, report to Reception and do not wander around the yard.

Checklist

✓ find a good teacher
✓ follow their instructions
✓ the right horse
✓ taking your first lesson

Start right

Make sure you are dressed safely and comfortably, and do what your instructor tells you. Horses are prey animals and, no matter how well trained, they can potentially be dangerous to the unknowledgeable because of their natural instinct to run away from danger if frightened. If you follow your teacher's instructions you will almost certainly be fine – but there is risk in any equestrian sport.

Meeting your instructor

If you did not meet your instructor on your first visit, you will do so now. They should explain what goes on so that you are familiar with the routine. You may also have the chance to meet other learners who will share their experiences with you.

The more novice you are as a rider, the better teacher you need. You should always check whether your instructor is qualified to teach. Not all of them are but there are many excellent unqualified teachers. At the very least, your teacher should be experienced and recommended by others before you allow yourself to be taught.

A good teacher, in whom you have complete faith, makes all the difference. Once you have started, it is important to try to stay with the same teacher and horse for a while so that you build up a good relationship and progress logically. Remember to ask your instructor any obvious questions before you start your lesson – you will certainly have masses to ask afterwards and a good teacher will not regard any question as 'silly'.

Your first mount

A good first horse will be an experienced 'schoolmaster' that has already taught many people to ride. He will be quiet, steady and tolerant, and seem to understand the importance of taking his rider very slowly during the first few lessons. Treat him kindly and ask permission before

Booking your first lesson can give you quite a kick – of the right kind!

giving him a titbit. Most horses like mints, but some schools have a 'no titbits' policy as overdoing them can cause some horses and ponies to start nipping out of disappointment if a treat is not forthcoming.

Familiarize yourself

Watch carefully what goes on at the stables on your first and subsequent visits, so that you get to know whether your horse will be in his stable or in the yard and how to find him; whether you will be involved in grooming and tacking him up; where you will be expected to mount him and how this works; and where each part of the lesson takes place.

If you are borrowing a hat and/or body protector, familiarize yourself with where these are kept. Find out who you should talk to about ensuring that you have the right size and that the fastenings are adjusted correctly.

Your first lesson

If you want your lesson in complete privacy with no one watching, say so in advance. This is understandable and not unknown in novice riders.

You should have booked a private lesson for your first time, and several subsequent ones. The instructor needs to give you all their attention, so it is worth paying the slightly higher fee for this type of one-to-one lesson.

If you are a complete beginner, you will probably have your teacher at one side and maybe a helper on the other. If you have a little experience, the teacher alone will probably take you.

You may well be put on the lunge: this means that your horse will be on a long rein that runs from his head to the teacher's hand, and the teacher can walk close to you or further away as they instruct you in your seat or body position on the horse and how to give the aids or signals to the horse.

Don't worry about being asked to do things that concern you. Your teacher will take things very slowly, staying with you and giving you plenty of time to take everything in.

Do you have?

Make sure you have equipped yourself with:
- hat
- gloves
- boots
- jodhpurs or tough trousers.
(See also pages 110–111.)

Mounting your horse

The bond between horse and human has been recorded throughout history. A real partnership takes time to develop and you must understand something of horse psychology. Horses are very strong and potentially dangerous if frightened, wrongly handled or abused. Properly treated, the horse offers a unique friendship, a very special 'someone' to care for. Around horses, you need to be calm, firm and positive.

Checklist
✓ the correct approach
✓ safety checks
✓ mounting and dismounting

Approaching your horse

Never walk up to a horse and try to pat him on the head. Horses dislike this unnatural action (they never do it to each other) – and so do dogs and children. Stroking the horse's neck in front of his withers will relax him. Talk to him and let him sniff you.

Always approach from the front and be sure your horse is aware of your presence. Say his name and never frighten him by quick, unexpected movements. Avoid feeding titbits on a regular basis. Your horse will come to expect these and may react with a kick or a bite if you fail to deliver. If you do offer a food treat, always keep your hand, fingers and thumb flat to avoid being chewed by mistake.

Safety check

Before you mount, your instructor will need to:
• Ensure that the horse is suitable for you and the tack properly adjusted.
• Tell you how the lesson is going to be conducted.
• Check that the girth is tight enough to mount and that the stirrups are down ready for mounting.
• Explain all these things to you.

Mounting from a mounting block

A mounting block will be about the height of your mid-thigh. It is easier to mount this way, better for the saddle, and better for both your and your horse's backs.

Your instructor will hold your horse next to the block. Stand on the horse's left. Take up the reins, put your left foot in the stirrup, straighten your knee and swing your right leg up and over your horse's back, taking great care not

to kick him. Put your right foot in the stirrup and lower yourself gently down into the saddle. Many people sit down first, then put the right foot in the stirrup.

Mounting from the ground

Although quite an effort when you aren't used to it, you need to be able to do this in case you are ever alone with nothing to stand on to mount. Just follow the sequence shown (right).

You should hold the reins with a gentle but definite contact on the bit and shorten the right rein (away from you) slightly more than the left one. This will turn the horse's head a little away from you so that if he does move off his body will come towards you and you can still mount – and not be left hopping after him on one leg! Your teacher should stand on the horse's right and pull down on the right stirrup to counteract your weight in the left one. If this isn't done, it is more uncomfortable for your horse.

Ideally, you should be able to steady and support yourself by placing your right hand on the horse's wither. Many people, though, prefer to hold the saddle to help until they are more proficient. If so, hold it in the middle (at its 'waist') on the side away from you. Never hold the cantle (rear arch) to mount as this can badly twist the saddle tree (framework).

Although our photographs show a learner rider mounting without help, don't worry about having to do this at first. Your teacher will certainly help out if you are having difficulties. If you do have, say, an old injury or some kind of weakness, do tell your teacher. It will probably not mean you cannot ride and she will be understanding and helpful.

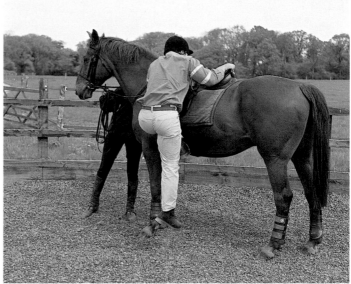

1 *Stand by the horse's left shoulder facing his tail. Hold the reins with your left hand and rest it on the horse's withers. Steady the stirrup with your right hand as you lift your left leg and put your foot well into the stirrup.*

2 *Hop round to face the horse's side and spring and push upwards with your right leg, holding the far side of the saddle in the middle, taking your weight on your left foot in the stirrup.*

3 *Lift your right leg high enough to avoid kicking the horse's rump and bring it over to the horse's right side, steadying yourself with your hands as you settle gently down into the saddle.*

4 *Lower yourself gently and put your right foot in the right stirrup. Hold the reins in both hands as shown by your teacher and assume the body position you will be taught.*

1 *Keeping hold of the reins and steadying yourself with your hands on the saddle pommel (front), take both your feet out of the stirrups. Lean forwards and swing your right leg up and back to the left.*

2 *Be sure not to kick the horse as you do this as this might cause him to move and throw you off balance, resulting in a fall.*

3 *Leaning slightly on the front of the saddle, with both legs down the horse's left side, allow yourself to drop down, at the same time pushing yourself slightly away from the saddle with your arms.*

4 *It is important that you bend your knees on landing to prevent jarring your joints.*

DO	DON'T
• Talk to your horse when mounting.	• Dig your toe into the horse while mounting – push it downwards instead.
• Keep hold of the reins while mounting, in case he moves.	• Bump down into the saddle, which may hurt or frighten the horse.
• When you have settled into position, pat him gently.	• Pull on the cantle of the saddle, as this may damage it.
• Check that your feet are straight in the stirrups.	
• Stand up in the stirrups to check they are even in length.	

Dismounting

Most riders not used to riding (and some who are, after a long ride) feel a little wobbly on landing from the saddle, which confirms that the muscles used in riding are different from those normally used every day.

When you land, immediately stroke your horse and talk to him to thank him. He will understand.

The first thing to do after this is to run your stirrups up their leathers: bring the reins forward over his head and link them over your arm at the buckle so that you have control of your horse and slide first one stirrup, then the other, up the back part of the stirrup leather by the eye at the top of the stirrup. When it reaches the stirrup bar, fold the stirrup leather back and down through the stirrup to hold it securely in place.

The second thing to do is to loosen your horse's girth a couple of holes to give him a breather and a more comfortable feeling. Do not loosen it so much that it is in danger of slipping around or back as you lead him back to his stable.

Depending on your yard's routine, your horse may now be going out in the field, into his stable or, after a short rest, be working again.

Unsafe dismounting methods

An old method of dismounting is to stand in the stirrups and bring the right leg over the horse's back level with the left, the foot of which is still in its stirrup. The rider then supports himself or herself on the saddle pommel and cantle with the left and right hand respectively, takes the left foot out of its stirrup and drops to the ground. This is now considered not the safest way to dismount because if the horse becomes startled and jumps about, or even moves a little, while the rider still has the left foot in its stirrup, he or she could become unbalanced and fall, catching the left foot in the stirrup and having a nasty accident.

Another old method, still sometimes used in some types of riding, is for the rider to swing the right leg over the horse's back and take it right to the ground, not removing the left foot from its stirrup till the right foot has landed. This could mean, again, that if the horse moves the left foot could become stuck in the stirrup and the rider could be caught up and hurt. In methods of riding such as Western, where larger, more bulky saddles are used, it has to be said that this is a more convenient method of dismounting. In the vault-off method usually taught in English-style riding, the rider would find it very difficult in a Western saddle.

It is sometimes seen in modern riding that a rider will quit both stirrups, then swing the right leg up and forward over the horse's neck and drop down to the ground with his or her back to the horse's side. This is asking for trouble because if the horse moves it could bump into the rider as he or she is dropping down, knocking them over, or, if the horse moves the other way, could leave the rider with no support during the dismount, causing a fall.

On the lunge

Lunge lessons form the basis of learning to maintain a correct position in the saddle. The rider need not bother about controlling the horse as the teacher will do this, making it easier for the rider to concentrate on their position. Lunge lessons are valuable throughout your riding life no matter how competent you become. It is common to get into bad habits without realizing it and lunge lessons really make you think and work.

✓ developing your seat
✓ the correct position
✓ feeling the movement
✓ balancing on the horse

Why no reins or stirrups?

Lunge lessons often involve riding without reins or stirrups. Reins and especially stirrups can actually hinder a rider from learning a correct and fully independent seat, not relying on either reins or stirrups to stay on, control the horse or sit correctly. Good riders can often be seen schooling horses without stirrups so that they can maintain a deeper seat. Somehow, just lengthening the stirrups does not have quite the same effect.

Using the reins to keep yourself on, except in dire emergency, is very bad horsemanship and can really hurt the horse's mouth, destroying his trust in you and teaching him in no uncertain terms to ignore your rein aids.

As a beginner or novice, however, your horse will probably be wearing a neckstrap for you to hold on to, or you can hold the front (pommel) of the saddle, if you prefer. At this stage, you will feel more secure if you have stirrups and your teacher will almost certainly teach you this way.

The correct position

- You should sit upright on the horse without being stiff, and look straight ahead, not down at the horse.
- Your legs should hang down, with your feet resting on the ball of the foot in the stirrups.
- Let your weight fall down the back of your leg into your heel. Your whole legs should be relaxed and dropped down the horse's sides. Do not make a conscious effort to keep your legs touching the horse: constant leg contact can make the horse less responsive to light leg aids.
- Your knees should be bent and the stirrup length adjusted to suit: too short is generally better than too long at this stage.

Seen from the side, you should be able to drop a vertical line down from the rider's ear through his shoulder, hip and heel. Ideally, the elbow should be held further back than this, resting at the hip.

This rider is a little crouched and looking down but otherwise making a good effort. Think of stretching up and dropping down from the waist, allowing the weight of your legs to drop down through your heels, and keeping them below your hips.

• Your arms should hang naturally at your sides, with your elbows bent and held at your hips, not out in front of you. Your hands should rest just above the wither or pommel (depending on your forearms' natural length), with your thumbs uppermost and your little finger at the bottom.

First steps

Your teacher will explain all this while leading you to allow you to get used to the horse's movement. At first, it is best to lean forward a little rather than back while you find your balance. You may be asked to practise starting and stopping a few times, until you have learned how to stay in balance with your horse as he does this.

Your teacher will lead you around on the lunge rein until you feel confident and will then give you a longer rein to walk out on to a circle. They will probably tell you how to make little turns in your line so that you can see that you are influencing the horse and getting him to do what you want.

If this is your first lesson, you may not be asked to trot, and after half an hour will probably have had enough. Riding uses completely different muscles to any other pursuit and can be quite tiring.

Using the reins

Holding the reins correctly will help you to communicate instructions directly to the horse. Remember that the horse's mouth is very sensitive and the lighter your use of the reins the better. Unfortunately, not all riding school horses are responsive to the bit, as they have experienced numerous riders pulling at their mouths, which have become somewhat insensitive.

Top tip

Breathing correctly when riding is most important. It is surprising how many riders hold their breath while concentrating on what they are trying to learn. This makes you tense and the horse will sense this. Stay relaxed and breathe normally.

Walking

The walk is an important gait and one the rider needs to move his or her seat with according to the horse's back movements. You need to learn to make your horse walk smartly but not rushing, using intermittent leg aids (squeezes) but do not nag at every stride or he will ignore you. Some horses have a naturally fast walk, others slow, with varying lengths of stride.

Checklist
- ✓ footfall at walk
- ✓ aids for walk
- ✓ the rider's position
- ✓ hand and seat movement
- ✓ going with the horse

About the walk

In the walk, the horse lifts and sets down each foot separately, in the following sequence:

Left hindleg
Left foreleg
Right hindleg
Right foreleg

These four steps (beats) make up one stride. The walk is called a four-beat, lateral gait because the horse moves the two legs on one side first (which make up a lateral pair), then the other two. The walk should be loose and supple with the horse moving freely forward and in balance.

Aids for the walk

As your teacher leads the horse forward, or asks him to move into walk on the lunge, they will probably ask you to give him the aids or signals for walk. Just give a gentle inward squeeze (not a backwards kick) with both legs to go from halt to walk. Remember to open your fingers on the reins a little so as not to give a stop aid inadvertently as the horse moves off, which would confuse him.

Position at the walk

A mistake many riders make, usually because they do not have the confidence to let the horse walk on freely, is to lean forward with short reins and their hands too far in front of them.

1 *The horse's left hindleg takes the weight of horse and rider. The weight is then transferred onto the left foreleg.*

2 *Weight is transferred from the left foreleg to the right hindleg.*

The correct seat (or position) for the walk is for the rider to sit upright (or very slightly forward if a novice) with the back flat, the chest raised and the elbows resting lightly at the hips, not several centimetres in front of them. There should be a very light contact through the reins to the bit in the horse's mouth.

Your heels should be underneath your seat, so that when you glance down (without leaning forward) you can just see the tip of your toe beyond your knee. In effect, you need to sit on your seat bones (the bottom of your pelvis), rather than your buttocks.

Your hands move with his head...

You will need to move your hands in time with the horse's head and neck movements. In walk, the horse's head swings slightly up and down with each lateral pair of legs, to help him balance. You need to 'go with' this movement with your hands. As a foreleg lands the head will drop a little, so you need to move your hands forward slightly, taking them back a little as the head rises again, to drop again with the next foreleg. This is easier to do than it sounds!

...and your seat moves with his back

It is important to learn eventually to feel the movements of the horse's back underneath you. This takes some practice and can only really be learnt by completely relaxing and loosening the muscles of your buttocks and legs. In this way,

Types of walk

Free walk The horse moves forward unrestricted, stretching his head and neck down. The rider has a very light contact on the bit.
Medium walk The horse is more 'up together'. The rider maintains contact with the reins and uses a stronger leg aid.
Collected and extended walks More advanced movements, these walks require the trained horse to shorten or lengthen his stride considerably.

you will feel the horse's back swinging beneath your seat. As the left hindleg moves forward, the left side of the horse's back will dip, and as the right hindleg moves forward the right side will dip.

Stretch up from your waist, drop your seat and legs, and allow your pelvis to swing gently with the movement of the horse's back.

Co-ordination

With this kind of co-ordination of hand and seat, which you will get used to in time, you will truly go with your horse and he will maintain a loose, supple, ground-covering walk.

3 *The right hindleg, having taken the weight, pushes this to the right foreleg ready for the sequence to begin again.*

4 *The rider's hands should contuniue to move in time with the head and neck movements of the horse.*

Trotting

Trotting can be tricky but a good school will give you the best horse for this job. He will be patient, tolerant and trot steadily, obeying the vocal commands of your teacher. It is easier to learn the trot at a medium speed. Slow trotters are difficult for beginners and fast ones can be frightening until you have developed the body 'feel' and balance to be able to go with them.

About the trot

In the trot, the horse moves his legs in diagonal pairs, in the following sequence:

Left foreleg and right hindleg together
Moment of suspension (in the air)
Right foreleg and left hindleg together
Moment of suspension

This produces a springing gait as the horse springs from one diagonal pair of legs to the other. The trot is called a two-beat diagonal gait, with two beats being one stride. To be a comfortable ride, the trot should be smooth and supple, not stiff and jarring.

Aids for the trot

These are the same as the aids for moving from halt to walk (see pages 122–123): a gentle inward squeeze with both legs and an opening of your fingers on the reins.

Starting to trot

Your teacher will lead the horse at this stage and run with you, until you have become accustomed to the movement of the trot and learned how to keep your weight forward as the horse's more exaggerated steps throw you up and forward.

You can hold on to the neckstrap or pommel of the saddle to help you at this stage. As the horse is asked to trot, keep your weight forward a little and allow yourself to

1 *Lean slightly forward and let yourself softly bump up and down, maybe supporting yourself on the horse's neck with your hands. Once you get the feel of the gait and learn to keep your balance, you will find that it's not so difficult.*

2 *The next step is to learn to rise up and down in time with the horse's gait. As the horse goes 'one, two, one, two' you go 'up, down, up, down'. It's easier if you don't rise too far as, if you do, you might come down with a rather hard bump at first.*

bounce in the saddle. To start with, ride just a few steps of trot at a time, until you feel ready to do more each time. Once you have felt what trotting is all about, have a rest and talk it through with your teacher.

You can sit to a slow trot by allowing yourself to bump gently in the saddle to the horse's movements. Eventually, you will be able to soften this feel by allowing the small of your back to go forwards and backwards, hollowing and flattening your back as you go down and up with the horse. This is a movement known as the 'pelvic tilt' and is familiar to anyone who dances or does bodywork such as yoga or Pilates. As your back hollows a little as the horse lands, the wings of your pelvis (commonly but incorrectly known as the hips) move forward, flattening again as he moves upwards in suspension. Don't worry about this – it will come with time.

Learning to rise

You'll notice that for most ordinary riding, people rise up and down in the trot. This is less tiring and is called 'posting'. On one diagonal, as the horse pushes you up, control your rise so that your pelvis moves more forwards than upwards (the pelvic tilt again) and instead of dropping down just think of sitting gently. So, you are going 'forward, sit, forward, sit' and so on, moving forward and up on one beat and sitting on the next. Relax, and don't try too hard.

As you become more proficient at this rising trot, as it is called, which will take only a few lessons, try to start thinking of controlling your legs more. They should remain as still as possible and near vertical, lying just behind the girth of the saddle. Do not stiffen them, though. Think of dropping your legs through supple ankles as you rise and

Little and often

To perfect the art of trotting, both sitting and rising, requires plenty of practice, so use the little-and-often maxim. Keep practising moving from walk to trot and back to walk, and then to halt. You will soon become confident that you can stay with your horse's movements as he takes you through the transitions between walk and trot.

keeping your feet close to your horse's sides. As you sit, slightly tuck your bottom in and let your weight go down through your heels, again keeping your feet and legs gently close to your horse's sides.

Watch your position

• Keep your head up and look ahead between your horse's ears.
• Keep your hands low near the withers and stable, not rising and falling.
• Do not allow your legs to slide forwards and your weight to fall backwards.
• Try not to push yourself up with your legs, but rather drop your legs as you rise.
• Try to keep your legs back behind the girth and still, not flapping in and out or back and forth.
Like everything else, this takes practice, but you will get the knack quicker if you think of keeping your legs still and dropped down.

DO

• Keep your weight forward when rising to the trot.
• Go with the horse's movements.
• Find the rhythm of the trot, and rise and sit with it.
• Maintain your balance and sit straight.
• Keep your hands low.
• Slow down if your horse is trotting too fast and try again.

DON'T

• Allow your weight to fall backwards.
• Raise your hands and slide your legs forward.
• Lose balance and start bumping down on the saddle.
• Lose heart if it doesn't work first time – just try again.

Cantering

A well-schooled, smooth, balanced canter is heaven to ride if the rider is also up to the standard of a horse able to produce it. You need to have acquired the knack of dropping your legs and weight gently and softly down into the saddle but stretching your upper body up and keeping it vertical (not swinging backwards and forwards) as the horse rocks beneath you. This section will give you some help with this.

Checklist
✓ footfall at canter
✓ incorrect canters
✓ aids for canter
✓ going with the movement
✓ riding the gallop

About the canter

The canter is a three-time, diagonal gait in which there are three distinct beats followed by a moment of suspension, when all four feet are off the ground.

In canter, the horse uses what is described as a 'leading leg'. This depends on whether he is cantering to the right ('on the right rein') or the left ('on the left rein'): when moving to the right, the horse will appear to point the way with his right foreleg, and vice versa, and is said to be 'on the right lead' or 'on the left lead'. Because of this difference, there are two sequences of footfalls in canter.

Cantering to the right, the sequence is:
Left hindleg
Right hindleg and left foreleg together
Right foreleg (leading leg)
Moment of suspension

Cantering to the left, the sequence is:
Right hindleg
Left hindleg and right foreleg together
Left foreleg (leading leg)
Moment of suspension

1 *The rider uses his right leg to encourage the horse forwards and maintain the canter.*

2 *As the horse stretches forward into his stride the rider has also stretched forward with his hand to follow the movement.*

Sitting to the canter

The trick of sitting to the canter and not banging about in the saddle is to sit up with your upper body straight and drop your legs down. Move with the horse's up-and-down, rocking movement by allowing your thighs to rise and fall naturally with him from your hip joints. As the horse's forehand rocks up, your hip joints flex/close slightly and your thighs rotate upwards; as it drops, the joints open again and your thighs rotate downwards.

This does take practice but a schoolmaster horse with a rock-steady, rhythmic canter will help you to get it.

Aids for the canter

First make sure that the horse is moving forward well in trot. To canter to the right, as the horse approaches a right-handed corner push your inside (right) hip/seat bone and shoulder forward and ask him for a slight bend to the right by gently increasing your contact on the right rein – just a squeeze of your right fingers should do. Then brush your outside (left) leg back and nudge the horse strongly behind the girth, while sitting safely in the saddle. A responsive and well-trained horse should strike off directly into canter. To canter to the left, reverse the aids.

The important thing is not to lean too far forward, grip with your legs, or allow the horse just to trot faster and faster. As you are still practising these things on the lunge,

your teacher will correct these points and, of course, control the horse. A good lunge horse will canter to the verbal command 'can-TER'. Once you have got the hang of it after a few repetitions on the lunge, you won't find cantering unnerving when you ride solo.

Once the horse has moved into canter, your aim is to allow your body to move forward in rhythm with the horse's movements. Cantering is a very comfortable gait for the rider on a schooled horse, once the necessary balance has been mastered.

Galloping

The gallop is a faster version of the canter and is actually quite an easy gait to sit to. It is level, smooth, and the horse is normally going too fast to buck! Your problem may be stopping, but if the horse takes off and you can't pull him up, you can perhaps rest a little easier in the knowledge that all you have to do is sit there and lean forward, balanced, until he gets where he wants to be – strangely, most horses do not run towards the fields and their friends but back towards their stables. Sit up and hang on to the saddle as he stops, because he may drop to a halt suddenly or swerve.

If you have more experience and confidence, the best thing to do is turn the horse in decreasing circles until he has to stop. Then walk on as though nothing had happened – it is useless to reprimand him for stopping.

3 *At the end of the stride the rider's weight is more upright to allow the horse to rebalance ready to make the next stride.*

4 *The horse is now ready to repeat the sequence.*

Coming off the lunge

This is a big day – the first time you ride and control your horse entirely on your own. Your teacher will be there, of course, and it will be done in gradual stages – but you are off the lunge! Your teacher will correct any faults that now creep in and probably get you to perform certain manoeuvres or 'school movements', such as circles, changes of direction and serpentines that cannot be done on the lunge.

Checklist

✓ riding solo
✓ working on turns and circles
✓ changing direction
✓ riding school movements

You are entitled to feel a great sense of achievement at this point – riding alone with no one holding your horse but you!

Letting go

At the point where your teacher considers that you are ready to ride 'unattached', your problems may be more psychological than physical. You will be riding your schoolmaster horse, probably a familiar friend by now. You know how to mount and dismount, move off, walk, trot, maybe canter, move from one gait to another and stop, doing all this on both reins.

Your teacher will unfasten the lunge rein and walk next to you, maybe with a hand on your reins initially, but will soon let go and walk a metre or so away from you. You will have learnt how to keep the horse on a circle on the lunge without your teacher having to steer him, so the absence of the lunge rein should make little difference. Your teacher may gradually walk a little further away from you and may get you to ride circles of different sizes.

Practising circles

The smaller the circle, the more difficult it is and the more active and precise you need to be to keep the horse moving around your line. Circles are a very basic exercise, but require a surprising amount of time and effort to master completely. Most people initially ride potatoes!

Keep your inside hip and shoulder forward a little, your outside leg back a little, and gently ask your horse – by means of little squeezes on the inside rein – to flex (bend) his head and neck slightly in the direction he is going. Your outside leg prevents the hindquarters from swinging out, while the inside leg prevents the horse falling in on the circle. Try circles at walk, trot and maybe canter, on both reins, using the same principles. In a school, circles are usually ridden in sizes of 20m (66 ft), 15 m (49 ft) and 10 m (33 ft).

Riding school movements

Keep the following thoughts in your mind when riding any exercise in an arena:

• Maintain forward movement, rhythm and balance.
• Keep to your line.
• Your hands control the horse's balance and steering.
• Your legs control the hindquarters and the horse's speed.
• Look where you want to go and your horse will almost certainly go there.

Changing the rein

Probably the first new movement your teacher will show you will be how to change the rein (change direction). For this, you have to be able to steer your horse. This is very important and worth spending time on to get the basics properly established before moving on.

Imagine you are walking on the right rein. You are coming to the end of a short side of the arena. To turn your horse down the long side, you give the usual aids but instead of stopping them when he is on the long side continue them and look diagonally down the school to the far corner. The horse will turn on to the diagonal line, along your line of sight. At this point, stop asking him to turn and ride him straight. As you approach the corner, give the aids to turn left, the horse will go round the corner – and you have done it. You are now on the left rein.

Serpentines

Serpentines are loops across the arena. They are simply combinations of bends (all bends are part of a circle) and straight lines, so help you to learn control, steering, bends, riding straight and changes of direction – all excellent riding practice.

No wonder this rider is grinning. His horse is walking out confidently under his instruction and he is controlling both the horse and himself.

Top tips

• Riding circles is made easier if you learn to look about a quarter of the way around your circle to where you want to go, and keep looking on around your line until you want to come off the circle. It is amazing how horses follow your eyes and tend to go where you look.
• It's best to look up, too. If you look down at your horse all the time he can feel pressurized and may actually move less freely.
• Another tip for circles is to imagine a railway track laid out on the ground in a perfect circle and that you are riding around in between the two rails.

Class lessons

It can be great fun, having your first class lesson. A gentle introduction to having several other horses and ponies in the arena with you would be to share a lesson with one or two others. Riders of similar levels of abilities will be grouped in one class so you won't have to do anything too difficult – but you have to try new things or you will never progress. After a couple of lessons off the lunge, you will be ready to join a class.

Checklist
✓ avoiding accidents
✓ arena etiquette
✓ 'formation' riding
✓ different classes

Class and arena etiquette

There are certain rules to be observed concerning riding in company. These are so that everyone knows the correct procedure, and collisions and other accidents are less likely.

• When you want to enter an enclosed indoor school, listen for horses nearby, knock or call out to ask permission.

• If you want to leave the arena, wait until the outside track is clear, then cross it at the entrance and leave, closing the gate or rail behind you.

• We ride left hand to left hand in an arena (similar to driving on the right-hand side of the road).

• When riding in 'open order' (not 'as a ride' in a line, but where you wish), the fastest-moving horse has the right to the outside track. So, for example, if someone is cantering

Beginners sometimes have a helper each, with the teacher in charge. This gives confidence and helps you to learn manage riding etiquette.

and the others are trotting and walking, those in the slower gaits leave the track and come on to the inside track (about a metre in from the outside track) or work in the main area of the school.

• If jumping, it is normal to call out 'jumping' so that people can keep out of your way and avoid an accident.

• If you want to chat to your friends, come into the centre of the arena and talk quietly.

• The arena supervisor or riding teacher is to be obeyed implicitly – no arguing!

Use your head

For the first time, in a class lesson you will not have your teacher's full attention and will have to be alert at all times to make sure you do not cause accidents. You will soon get used to the different ways of running a ride if you stay alert.

Even with only one other rider, you can begin to learn formation riding, drill patterns and riding in pairs whilst considering your partner and controlling your own horse. Great fun!

Class movements

There are various ways of teaching in a class. Some parts of the time will be involved in teaching general matters to everyone, and those present work 'as a ride', performing manoeuvres decided by the teacher. In each lesson there will be times when you work individually: for example, the leader of the ride may be asked to canter around the track to the rear of the ride, then the new leader will do the same and so on, until everyone has cantered alone.

Rides may be split into two and various exercises performed, which will be explained to you. Rides may be asked to number off in twos from the front of the ride, each rider calling out in turn 'one', 'two', 'one', 'two' from front to back. Then the 'ones' will, say, track left at A and the 'twos' will track right, forming two rides, and perform further manoeuvres according to the teacher's instruction.

Class sizes

Some riding schools run quite large classes where no real individual instruction is given, and most people feel that these are a waste of time and money. Rides of six or less are best for novice riders, as reasonable individual attention can be expected. The advantage to the client of class rides is that they are cheaper than private lessons.

Class types

There will be beginner classes, novice classes, intermediate classes and advanced classes. There could also be flatwork/dressage classes and jumping classes for different levels. Get details from your school's office or reception.

Going further

Weekend classes are very popular but there may also be evening classes that you can take to improve your skills more quickly. As you progress, you will find that there are classes in the indoor school, outdoor arena, maybe on a cross-country course of varied jumps, in a showjumping field, and also hacking or riding out in the surrounding area. Riding schools often hold shows and you can hire one of their horses on which to compete.

Fast cantering and galloping

You do not have to do anything on a horse that you do not want to do. Fast gaits are needed if you want to compete across country and in show jumping or working hunter classes, and if you want to enjoy active hacking over varied terrain. If you do not feel confident to do a particular thing, however, do not do it. Nervous riders can lead to anxious horses (they aren't all schoolmasters) and this can lead to accidents.

Checklist
✓ the forward seat
✓ gathering speed
✓ control issues
✓ suitable ground conditions

Elements of the forward seat

The history of the forward seat is described on pages 18–19. Over the years, this seat (also sometimes called the jumping seat or the half seat) has been modified and is not now so exaggerated as formerly, except in the racing world.

• The rider has a slightly shorter stirrup than for flatwork – say two or three holes shorter on the stirrup leathers, depending on preference.

• The seat requires a saddle with forward-cut flaps to accommodate the shorter stirrup length and, therefore, the more bent knee.

• In fast canter and gallop, and for negotiating hazards and fences, the rider normally leans forward from the hip joints – not from the waist, which causes a round-shouldered posture – and maintains a flat back.

• The rider's seat is held lightly out of but close to the saddle seat.

• A good general guide is for the rider's shoulders to be held over their knees.

• The rider's weight is dropped down the legs into a flexible ankle, the lower leg remaining vertical and close to the horse's side.

• The upper arm is held vertically and there should be a straight line from the elbow, through the hand, down the reins, to the horse's mouth. A light but present contact is maintained. Horses who 'take hold' in faster gaits are not suitable for novice riders.

• The rider looks up and ahead between the horse's ears.

• In this position, the rider can quite easily remain balanced in fast gaits without being bounced up and down by the horse's back movements.

The modern forward seat is a little more vertical than in the past. The seat is held lightly in the saddle with more weight on the thighs and the shoulders above the knees.

DO	DON'T
• Drop your weight down your legs and hover above the saddle. • Balance on your thighs.	• Lean too far forward or lift your seat far out of the saddle, as this makes you insecure. • Hold on to the reins for security. This encourages some horses to pull when going fast and can be the start of loss of control.

Getting used to it

Your teacher will give you a feel for a bit of speed in the indoor school or outdoor arena, where you are safely fenced in, probably asking you to encourage the horse to move on a bit down a long side or across the diagonal.

A good way to learn the seat is to ride in 'hover seat' at trot and slow canter (once again, different muscles come into play). When you've got the hang of it, you will probably be given a steady horse and taken into a large outdoor arena or small field to try a fast canter, and on from there according to your level.

Frequently asked question

 What do I do if my horse bolts?

 This is extremely unlikely. Riding school horses, especially schoolmasters, are chosen for their sensible temperaments. They are used to teaching people, and awkward horses prone to misbehaving are not used for clients, particularly beginners and novices. If the horse is going faster than you wish, give normal slowing and stopping aids – intermittent feels on the reins, sitting up more, lowering your seat into the saddle unless this is very uncomfortable, and vocal commands to 'whoa' or whatever the horse responds to. You can also turn the horse in a decreasing circle. To repeat: this is very unlikely to happen.

This rider is a little further forward than she needs to be for a moderate canter. A slightly more vertical position would be more secure.

Ground conditions

Fast gaits put much more stress on a horse's legs and should not be carried out on either hard or soft ground. Hard ground jars the legs and can lame the horse, while soft ground makes it difficult for him to lift his feet out of the going quickly enough and tendon and ligament strain can result. Never do fast work on stony or rough ground either, as the horse may bruise his feet and even fall.

Pole work

Pole work is an introduction to jumping, is fun and encourages athleticism and concentration in the horse. It helps you to build up confidence and overcome any apprehension about how a horse may react to an obstacle. It is also excellent for giving you a feel of lengthened and shortened strides in the horse as he adjusts his pace to avoid treading on the pole, gives you a target and makes you concentrate.

Checklist

✓ a course of poles
✓ lines of poles
✓ riding technique
✓ pole patterns

Cantering over poles, as here, is one of the best ways of getting a feel for what jumping is all about as you get a feel of having negotiated an obstacle in your path.

Raising the poles

You can have more effect on your horse's action if you raise the poles on brick-sized wooden blocks, or raise one end only on the ground-level retaining board surrounding the arena.

Line of poles

A good way to continue is with a line of poles – say, three to start with, progressing to six.

• With the poles spaced about 3 m (10 ft) apart, the horse is able to take one stride between each pole in trot.

• To trot over one pole per 'spring', space the poles just over 1 m (3 ft) apart – approximately one of your strides. Your teacher will help you to gauge whether this is too far apart or too close for your particular horse.

• To canter over poles, one per stride, they need to be about 3.3 m (11 ft) apart: again, horses' strides vary so your teacher might move the poles for different horses.

Single poles

Single poles placed on the ground in various positions around the arena can be very useful as a steering exercise. Practise taking the horse over one pole and then riding on to another. This is the start of the process of learning to ride a course of jumps.

So, think of the poles as jumps and try to ride them as a course. Work out the best route through them to give the horse an easy run – no sharp turns or doubling back, for instance. Aim for a logical, flowing course of single poles.

How to ride poles

You can ride poles in a normal, flatwork seat or in the forward seat. Generally, the more the horse needs to lengthen his stride and the faster he is going, the more likely

Poles can be used as markers for various exercises, giving you something to aim at. This helps you and your horse to adjust stride, improves accuracy and acts as a guideline.

that you will need the forward seat. Poles placed closer together call for more shortened paces and an upright, flatwork seat.

The secret of success is to keep your horse balanced by using the appropriate seat and riding him forward over the poles. If you look down at the first pole and wonder if the horse will go over it, he probably won't! Many horses appear to read their riders' minds and are influenced by them. For your introduction to poles and little jumps, you need a horse that knows his job and is willing to show you what to do – again, a true schoolmaster.

Corridors of poles

Laying out poles to form angled corridors – say, in a shallow Z-shape – down which you have to ride encourages accuracy, correct flexion of the horse's head and neck, and practises changes of direction. Ask the horse to stop part-way down, maybe rein back (back up) a step if you have learned this, walk on, turn, walk across the poles, maybe stop in the middle for control, walk on again and so on. Doing these things in trot is the next step, and much more difficult than you imagine.

Other patterns

Your teacher will have lots of good ideas for other patterns and uses of poles. They can be combined with traffic cones, barrels, upturned tubs and other gear to make obstacle courses and games, all aimed at having fun and improving your co-ordination, control and riding technique.

DO

• Try to ride over the centre of each pole to improve your skill and accuracy.
• Practise each exercise just a few times, as working over poles is tiring for the horse.

DON'T

• Increase your speed over the poles to maintain a rhythm.
• Allow your balance to drop behind the horse's movements.

Jumping small fences

It is most riders' dream one day to ride over fences and experience that wonderful feeling of 'flying' as your horse takes off. Jumping is an exhilarating feeling, but it will take practice. It is all about confidence, so no matter how keen you are, learn properly and take your time on a horse that will jump without argument and give you an enjoyable experience.

Checklist
✓ cross poles
✓ riding technique
✓ position over the jump
✓ simple jumps
✓ grids

Starting off

You will start off jumping over very low cross poles. These are two poles crossed one over the other and you jump – or rather hop – over the middle part, which will be about 30 cm (1 ft) high at the crossed point. This jump will automatically guide your horse psychologically towards its centre (given a choice, horses always jump the lowest part – they're not stupid) and they often treat it with some disdain.

Cross poles may form the final part of a line of poles

The pony has aimed for the middle (the lowest part!) of this little cross-pole fence and the rider can concentrate on folding down.

(your teacher will arrange this). You are already familiar with poles and raised poles, and the final hop over the cross poles is not a lot more effort. You may have heard that for jumping your stirrups need to be shortened, but for this tiny fence it is unnecessary. Sit in the correct seat and keep your horse moving forward, but do not rush him. If he is a schoolmaster, he will take you rather than vice versa.

A single jump

After jumping a cross pole at the end of a line of poles, you can jump one on its own.
• Keep the forward rhythm and balance all the way to the fence.
• Look 'through' the fence to some landmark in the distance.
• Keep the horse moving forward freely but not fast.
• Maintain your correct position.
• Let the horse find his own stride – that is, decide what to do with his feet and take off when he feels it is best.
• Feel with your body (by *not* looking down at the fence) what your horse is doing and go with his motion – and before you know it you will be on the other side.

Motivating your horse

How easy all this is depends a lot on the horse's temperament and natural way of going. It is easier to maintain rhythm and balance – vital for good jumping – on a forward-going horse than on a slower one. With the latter type, you will need to motivate him somehow, perhaps with a sharp canter, before attempting to jump.

This bigger cross-pole has placing poles before and after it to control the horse's stride so that he meets the fence and takes off at the right point and does not charge off after it.

Your position

If you are in the forward jumping position or half seat (see pages 132–133), all you need to do as your horse lifts his forehand to negotiate the cross poles is:

1 Fold your upper body *down* from the hip joints (*not* from your waist and *not* forward), as if you are trying to touch the horse's neck with your breastbone.

2 Move your hands diagonally forward down his shoulders towards his mouth, to give his head and neck room to stretch over the fence.

3 On landing, raise your upper body back again to your former position.

The next step

Once you are confident with cross poles, your teacher will probably set up a single pole at the same height as the cross pole – that is, a pole straight across between the jump stands at the same height as the crossed part of the cross pole. They may place a pole beneath it as a ground line, which makes things easier for the horse.

Approach in the same way as for a cross pole, in the jumping position/half seat, looking ahead through the fence, and folding down, not forward, pushing your seat back a little.

When you are confident over cross poles and single poles, your teacher will raise them slightly, maybe setting ground lines and placing poles (poles set at a distance to control

Problems

Difficulties inevitably arise from time to time, but don't dwell on them. Think about what happened, then try again. Ask yourself:

• Am I in balance?

• Am I being left behind the horse's movements?

• Am I moving too far forward?

These crucial factors will influence whether the horse takes off too early, too late, or not at all!

your horse's stride into them). You will then be able to say that you can jump small fences correctly and confidently.

Grids

Grids are lines consisting of poles and small fences. There will be a pole to start, then a cross pole, then maybe another pole and a little straight pole fence at the end. A grid of four to six cross poles is excellent for giving you balance and confidence. Your teacher will arrange the grid and decide what combination or type of jump is best for you and your horse. You are now well on your way to jumping larger fences with confidence.

Jumping larger fences

The progression from small fences and grids should be so gradual that you barely feel it. Your teacher should take you slowly, concentrating on giving you a willing, sensible horse, and working to maintain your correct jumping position. It is fun to jump little cross-country fences outdoors. This will give you an excellent grounding for negotiating larger fences, teach you more and give you a real thrill of achievement.

Checklist
✓ riding to the jump
✓ helping the horse
✓ the horse decides take-off
✓ riding away from the jump
✓ cross-country jumps
✓ jumping nerves
✓ safety

Developing style

Style is very important and, as a beginner and novice, you may find it difficult at first not to get 'left behind' (lurched backwards) over a fence, while you are still getting used to the feel of jumping. Practise the forward seat, and hovering in canter (see pages 132–133).

The approach

The approach to a fence is very important. If you can master a balanced, forward and consistent, rhythmic stride into the fence, the rest will be easy.

To balance your horse, you need to keep his head up by raising your hands and encourage his hindlegs to come up with more energy underneath him by stronger use of your legs, so that he can support his own weight more effectively. This enables him to lighten his shoulders, so that his strides are bouncier and free. In this way, the horse will find it easy to jump the fence.

If the horse is allowed to put his head down, his weight and balance will be too far forward on his forehand and he will not be able to jump so well, or will produce a 'flat' jump. The horse needs to form an arc (known as the 'parabola') over the jump, which, in itself, will produce the width, height and reach needed for larger fences.

Seeing a stride

Always wait for the fence to 'come to you' – do not try to 'see a stride' in order to get the horse to take off in a particular place. Striding will never be consistent if you increase pace or slow down. Just practise a forward, consistent, balanced canter into each fence – then where you

This rider has folded down well, not forward, and her hands are down, allowing the horse to arc over this fence.

Safety first

- Always check your girth before jumping.
- Wear gloves to protect your hands.
- Use a body protector and ensure that your hat is fastened securely, in case of a fall.

The teacher instructs as the rider negotiates a small drop fence, sitting correctly fairly upright so that she does not tip forward on landing.

Top tip

If you feel nerves creeping in, remember that the fence looks bigger to you (especially when you are on the ground) than it does to the horse.

are becomes irrelevant because the horse will decide where to take off. In effect, you decide the speed and direction, the horse decides when to jump. You just fold down as he rises and come up again as he starts to land over the fence.

Landing

Do not breathe a huge sigh of relief because you've got over the fence and then allow the horse to 'collapse in a heap'. Keep looking ahead in your forward seat (try not to bang the saddle – the horse's back – with your seat as you land) and maintain your pace and rhythm. After all, there may be another fence ahead or around a bend.

Cross-country riding

Starting with simple fences such as logs on the ground, you can progress to other small fences such as straw bales, small ditches and hedges, posts and rails, and then fences going up and down slopes.

Cross-country riding is all about balanced and controlled speed over fences – it should not be done flat out but in a consistent, faster rhythm than over showjumps. Because of the faster pace, you will need to shorten your stirrup leathers and ride with a strong leg, while sitting forward and in balance with your horse.

Sit up and hold your horse together as he jumps the different fences, but do 'give' forward with the reins as he jumps, otherwise you will restrict him too much. Your teacher will advise you how to approach the more specialized fences.

Rider nerves

There are occasions when the rider comes towards the fence with good intentions but, as it gets nearer, they communicate panic to the horse, who obligingly stops!

Do not worry if this happens to you – everyone experiences it at some stage. However, it may be an indication that you are not yet quite as ready to be brave as you thought – or, if you are, you may just need someone to tell you to get on with it.

Riding on roads

It is amazing how many riders spend their hours in the saddle just riding in an arena. Even riding around a cross-country course or jumping field (not necessarily jumping) is better than this. All riders should aim to help keep open local rights of way, but the problem is that to reach them some road riding is usually needed. Today, most motorists were not brought up with horses, so what is the best way to cope?

Checklist
✓ rules of the road
✓ visibility equipment
✓ slippery roads
✓ dealing with situations

Keep well to the side, according to your national road laws,
concentrate on road conditions and behave safely and courteously.

Basic rules

- Observe the motorist's code for your country and ensure that you do not inconvenience drivers.
- Always keep to the correct side of the road.
- Wear high-visibility clothing after dark and even in poor daylight.
- Be polite and thank drivers who slow down for you. Remember that they will not be able to see your acknowledgement other than in their mirror when they are past you, as you are well above their height.
- Do not ride more than two abreast at any time. If the road is narrow, stay in single file.
- The less experienced riders should stay on the inside (furthest from the traffic), ideally protected by an experienced horse and rider if there is room.

Be safe, be seen

High-visibility clothing (available for both horse and rider) is essential whenever you are on a public road, and a light (usually on the stirrup nearest the traffic) is vital when riding in poor natural light. Drivers will be travelling much faster than you are and may not see you until the last

Stay alert

Always stay aware of what is happening when riding on the roads. It is dangerous and irresponsible to be chatting to your friend, oblivious to the traffic around you.

moment. It is extremely dangerous to be out riding without being sure you can be seen clearly.

If you absolutely have to ride in the dark, use a stirrup light and fit reflective leg bands on the horse's legs, making sure his tail is short enough not to obscure them. The horse could wear a reflective sheet and you can get a reflective jacket and hat cover for yourself. These items really show up in the dark, but a strong light is your best safeguard.

Cyclists' gear is excellent. You can get lighted wrist bands to ensure your signals are seen, reflective gloves and cross-bands bearing lights for your body.

Problems

Any horse, however quiet, can become frightened in some situations, and on a road this can be dangerous.
- Assess each situation as it arises. For example, if confronted with a herd of cattle behind you, it may be best to stop, turn and face them, as your horse will then not feel he is being chased.
- If your horse becomes alarmed, turn into a gateway or stop and use hand signals to slow the traffic, then turn your horse's head away from the problem.
- When riding with others, allow at least one horse's length between you to avoid any risk of kicking.

Slippery surfaces

Some roads can be very slippery, making it difficult for the horse to keep his feet. Avoid roads like this if you can, and make a point of complaining about them – repeatedly, if necessary – to your local council. Ask your farrier to use anti-slip road nails in your horse's shoes to help.

If your horse does slip, loosen the reins and take your feet out of the stirrups, and sit very still and relaxed so that he can balance both of you. Quitting your stirrups also enables you to move your legs out of the way more easily if he slips over, allowing him to regain his balance unimpeded.

Experience and confidence

The more you can get out and about, the more you will build up your confidence. It is only by meeting and tackling different situations, such as tucking yourself into a gateway to allow traffic to pass, that you learn to think ahead. Always remember to acknowledge and thank considerate drivers. Conversely, if you have a problem with a driver and can note their registration number, report the incident to your local police, council and/or riding club.

Safety first

- Never ride out in fog or misty conditions. If you are out and fog looks likely, go home immediately.
- Dusk turns into night very quickly, especially in winter, so plan ahead and do not ride any further afield than absolutely necessary.

This is an excellent way to get a rider used to roadwork. Note the high-visibility clothing, and the companion between the pony and traffic.

Hand signals

Learn the basic hand signals used to indicate to drivers what you intend to do (check with your national equestrian organization). Give these well in advance and check that drivers behind you understand what you are about to do before you do it.

Hacking out

Hacking (riding out) is one of the highlights of riding a horse. There is no better way to enjoy the countryside than from the back of a horse. You can see so much more from up there! You are also less intimidating to wildlife, which stays much closer than if you were on foot or on a bike. You can hack alone or in company, a friend or partner can walk or run with you or ride a bike, and in some areas your dog can come, too.

Checklist
- ✓ practise your riding skills
- ✓ ride in company
- ✓ where to ride
- ✓ what to take
- ✓ long rides
- ✓ negotiating gates

Learning from hacking

You can continue to put many of the exercises and skills you have learned in the arena to good use on your rides, and will be amazed at how much you have achieved so far without realizing it. Repeat these exercises regularly while out hacking around the countryside – a more challenging situation than the arena – to enhance your skills further.

Alone or in company?

Do not ride out alone until you are experienced enough to do so (see pages 144–145). Ideally, having someone with you at all times is the safest option in case you have an unexpected accident. However, sometimes it is better to ride alone on a well-mannered horse than to ride with a selfish person who cares only for their own needs or who has a horse that does not behave.

Do you need permission?

Visit landowners and ask for permission to ride on their land. Many will say no, but not all. In this way you will build up a good relationship with them, which is well worth developing. Not all riders are as considerate as they might be and will give other riders a bad name.

Some countries have rights of way, some routes are 'permissive' (no actual right exists), and others have no actual rights of way at all but riding can take place on areas traditional to that country. Joining your local riding group is always a good idea.

Farmers may be encouraged to create paid farm rides, ideally linking ones, as a form of income for them and safer riding for equestrians.

Hacking away from traffic gives you more opportunity to chat and relax, although remember that horses can be startled by things other than traffic.

Sensible precautions

Always tell someone where you are going, make sure your horse's shoes are in excellent condition and dress for the weather. There is an old saying: walk the first mile out and the last mile home. This is to warm up your horse at the

Opening gates

1 *Position your horse next to the gate and lean over to open the catch. Maintain your balance and do not lean out too far.*

2 *Push the gate open. It must be wide enough for you to walk through easily. Make sure it does not swing back and hit your horse.*

3 *Turn the horse and ride up to the gate to secure the catch. Doublecheck that it is fastened securely before riding away.*

beginning of the ride and cool him down at the end. It is bad management to bring a horse home hot and sweating, makes more work for you and could give him a chill.

What to take with you

Take a well-charged mobile phone and basic horse-and-rider first aid kit with you. Make sure you have a contact telephone number on, say, a dog identity disc fastened to your horse's bridle or saddle, plus your own name, address and a contact number in your pocket.

Longer rides

If you are going to be out for several hours or more, you could take a snack and small bottle of water in a saddlebag. Remember your horse's needs, too. Dismount occasionally, run up your stirrups and loosen your girth, and take him on to some soft area to stale (urinate). Allow him to graze for a few minutes and, if possible, have a drink.

Grass verges

Beware of riding on grass verges unless you are sure they are safe. They may be littered with broken bottles or other debris thrown out by uncaring drivers, which can pose a real danger to horses. Close-mown, clearly ornamental verges should not be ventured on to except in an emergency.

Respect the countryside

• Shut all gates.

• Do not gallop across fields in which livestock are grazing.

• Walk around the edges of fields with growing crops – if possible, avoid these fields altogether until they have been harvested.

Riding alone

Most experienced riders love riding alone. It really gives you a chance to 'commune with nature', not to mention your horse. It is sometimes necessary to ride alone if there is no one else suitable with whom to ride. Many people do not take the trouble to train their horses to work alone in varied circumstances, and this greatly restricts their skills, their horse's education and maturity and their whole equestrian life.

Checklist
- ✓ know the basics
- ✓ keep control
- ✓ meet the challenges
- ✓ take precautions
- ✓ deal with problems

Practise the basics

Here, riding alone means alone anywhere: a few metres from your teacher in the arena, or many miles from home! There is a wonderful feeling of freedom once you are able to go it alone, but do not get carried away until you have mastered the basics. Practise will make perfect, so build up your confidence by repeating everything you have learned in the arena so far, until you are really sure that you know how to stop, start, steer and keep your balance at both walk and trot.

Broadening your horizons

Once you are safe to do so, you can ride out and about and make sure that you can cope as well in a field as in an arena. Your teacher will advise you on what to do or may even ride with you.

Keeping control

Constantly remind yourself how to stop and start the horse – you need to know that you can do this in all situations to build up your confidence. There are times when, for one reason or another, the horse may move a little more freely than you would like or feel able to cope with. Pull him up by sitting up a little and getting the stop reaction from him as you put pressure on the reins. Saying 'whoa' or whatever the horse responds to usually helps, too.

If you do not feel in control, pull the horse's head around so that he comes on to a circle. It is then much easier to regain control. Soften your hands as soon as he has stopped, stroke him and evaluate the situation.

Although riding in the middle of the road gives your horse a rest from the camber, make certain that there is no traffic around first, and move right to the side if any appears.

Common problems

Problem	Suggested solution
Horse attempts to buck with head down.	Pull his head up sharply using one rein and ride forward.
Horse is not moving forward.	Loosen the reins slightly and use your legs more strongly.
Horse is moving too quickly and/or is out of control.	Circle, stop and try again, shortening your reins slightly.

Difficult situations

• Never panic: the horse will sense this and become worried himself.
• Stay calm and talk quietly to the horse to calm him.
• If necessary, circle the horse to regain control.

Sit vertically going downhill to remain in balance and avoid over-burdening the horse's forehand, so helping to avoid tripping. It is safest to walk down hills and keep a light but present contact.

Problem or opportunity?

Inevitably there will be times when you become a bit anxious about how you are coping. Talk to your trainer about this aspect of your riding – together, you can work out a plan for how you should cope with a particular situation. Some horses may have their own little idiosyncrasies that need to be handled in a certain way, and learning how to do this will be a great help to you in the future and increase your confidence.

The best way to learn is to face up to and deal with a variety of situations. The more you attempt and come through successfully, the quicker you will learn to cope with the unexpected.

Common sense

Read and follow the advice given in the sections on hacking (pages 142–143) and riding on roads (pages 140–141). Make sure that you wear your hard hat, strong boots or shoes suitable for riding and, ideally, a body protector.

Riding out alone will usually mean that you have your own horse or have borrowed one from a very trusting friend. Riding centres almost never allow riders to hire a horse and go for a hack, because their insurance policies probably would not cover unsupervised riders in the event of a mishap – and, of course, they do not want you to have an accident either.

Riding in groups

Riding with others is fun. You get to know other people and horses. Sometimes, watching how a horse behaves with another rider helps you to decide whether or not you would want to ride him. All people and horses are different, with varying experiences, both good and bad, and, therefore, different attitudes to riding – or being ridden. Some horses do not get on and need to be kept apart, and so do a few riders!

Checklist
✓ riding with others
✓ building your confidence
✓ be considerate – expect consideration
✓ think ahead
✓ practise your skills

Riding out in company

Your first ride outside the arena will probably be with your trainer or someone from the riding school, and on a known route that is straightforward and safe. Ideally, you should be accompanied by a person who is aware of your capabilities. This should be someone who does not take risks but builds up your confidence and encourages you to lead the way where it is suitable and safe to do so. When you feel more capable, you can ride out with friends.

Riding in woods, for example, can be fun if there are good tracks through them, but be aware of low branches – you will need to lean forward far enough to ensure that you fit underneath without getting a nasty scrape or your hat being knocked crooked. Stop and evaluate the situation, and stay in walk if necessary. Just because other riders are going faster and jumping logs and ditches, it doesn't mean that you have to. Do not be chivvied into doing something you are not confident about as this can be dangerous. Look out for tree roots, which can cause the horse to trip. It is better to be cautious and make other people wait.

Be considerate

All members of the group need to be considerate of each other. It is just good manners, but where horses are concerned it is safer, too.
• If riding down a track wide enough for two horses abreast, for instance, don't ride in the middle so that the other rider is pushed to the side.
• If riding on roads and someone else's horse is not as good in traffic as yours, be prepared to ride on their outside, if you are experienced and the road is wide enough.

Riding in groups can be enjoyable or hair-raising depending on your company, both human and equine. Don't let your conversation distract you from safety issues, particularly on roads.

Road safety

Remember when riding on the road you will need to be aware of the motorist's code for your country and the hand signals to use (see pages 140–141).

Carry a whip

It is helpful to carry a whip when hacking out, to encourage the horse forward if he sees something he doesn't like and does not respond to your leg aids.

Many horses like to roll in water, rider and saddle notwithstanding. Be as sure as possible that the footing is safe, keep moving if it is soft, such as sand, and keep your horse's head up.

• Take your turn to dismount and open any difficult gates.
• At crossroads, don't filter across in a haphazard way, leaving one more nervous rider on the other side alone. Cross in pairs if you cannot all cross together.
• Don't canter and jump if this upsets someone else's horse, as an accident could ensue.

Expect consideration from others

• Sometimes, you may come across riders who think that everyone has to do what they want. This is not so – unless they happen to be the ride supervisor from your own riding centre.
• Your enjoyment and safety are just as important as other people's. If you are with a group of riders of similar standard, do voice your opinions as to what you would like to do and which route you should all take.
• A ride should function at the level of the least experienced, least confident rider. To do otherwise is dangerous. If that rider is you, speak up. Don't do anything that frightens you.
• If someone next to you constantly pushes you off the road or track, tell them to keep over and give you room – or slow your horse, go round the back of them, giving their horse

space in case he is a kicker, and come up on their other side. If they then push you to the other side, ride singly or with a different person.

Stay aware

You must learn to think ahead, and prepare for having to move off a track or keep into the side of the road if a car is coming. Adjust your balance when going up or down a hill: lean forward as you go up and stay vertical as you go down. Speed plays a part – keep it slow until you feel sufficiently in control to regulate how fast you go.

Keep practising

When riding out on a hack, you can practise some of the lessons you have learned in the arena. These are particular fun if you are with a ride supervisor and other riders of your level, as you can ride patterns around obstacles such as trees or practise school movements, stopping and starting, and even split-ride moves. Doing these things in a group really makes you aware of how far you have come and you will see that other riders have difficulties and concerns, too.

Problem solving

No one will ever tell you that riding is always easy and that you will never have problems. This is because horses are not machines: they have minds of their own, never forget anything and do not think like us. We are not all experts with horses and this can create misunderstandings. Horses can make decisions, though: if a horse just doesn't want to do something or doesn't like what you are doing, he may well tell you.

Checklist
✓ regaining control
✓ avoiding unnecessary risks
✓ dealing with situations
✓ solving jumping problems
✓ staying positive

Loss of control

If control is a problem, you will need to re-establish this – for instance, by slowing down as best you can through turning in a series of circles and shortening the reins until you can pull up. Remember that tugging continuously at the reins will not work: taking and giving as you circle will get a better reaction.

Play it safe

If your horse has been scared by something, talk to him, stroke him just in front of his withers, which is known to relax horses, and keep him on a shorter rein until you have both relaxed enough to continue as normal. If you think the problem could happen again, it may be better to dismount, run up the stirrups, take the reins over the horse's head and lead him home.

Learning 'on the job'

A good rider soon becomes aware of situations developing and responds to them. Tact and firmness are usually required to win any argument. Never lose your temper, however frustrating the situation.

Your attitude

Do not become discouraged when things go wrong. At some stage, they are bound to go better or worse than they did the last time. Just stop and think about why a problem occurred, talk about it with your teacher, and then set out to put it right with even more determination than before.

If a horse gives you a hard time, consider whether it is in fact you who is giving him a hard time. Remain calm, firm and positive and try to get him walking forwards.

This rider has got a little 'left behind the movement' when her horse has taken off by not folding down as he took off, but has given him freedom of head and neck by putting her hands forwards.

Jumping problems

Most problems in jumping occur because of lack of preparation by the rider.

A poor approach

This stops many horses because they do not get enough warning of what is expected. When jumping, this usually means that the approach has not been straight, so the horse has not had enough time to assess the fence he is supposed to be jumping. There may also not have been sufficient speed for the horse to jump the fence with ease, or the fence may be unsuitable or too big for the experience and ability of that horse-and-rider combination.

The thing to do is come in again, straight and with sufficient impulsion, looking ahead through the jump, not down at the horse or the fence. This usually puts things right for a successful jump.

Getting behind or in front of the horse's movement

This is also quite common. If the rider gets too far forward, it makes it difficult for the horse to lift his forehand. In this situation, he will eventually become demoralized. Sit up and drive him onwards positively – and control your own upper body as well.

The opposite can also happen – the rider sits too far back, then on take-off catches the horse in the mouth, and on landing crashes down on his back. He may forgive this once, but probably not twice. The horse will then either start refusing or bucking. To correct this, you need to improve your balance and technique before attempting to jump again – and start small.

The key to both these problems, apart from being in rhythm and balance with your horse, is always to fold down from the hips, not from the waist and not forwards.

Coping with a young or difficult horse

Riding at a good riding school or centre is an excellent way to start, to regain your nerve or technique after an unpleasant experience or after a long break. Such establishments will have several true schoolmaster horses to help you but there may come a time when you have to cope with young or difficult horses. The traditional, excellent system is for expert riders to train young horses and expert horses to teach novice riders.

Checklist

✓ riding youngsters
✓ being clear
✓ dealing with problems
✓ perseverance pays off
✓ why horses become difficult
✓ riding troubled horses

Starting off a youngster by leading him over poles introduces variety.

Aids

When you ride a young horse, your aids must be particularly clear and consistent but never rough. Use your voice in specific commands or to calm or reward, ride with a light seat, and always give the horse plenty of time and room to change direction – opening a rein to the inside without pulling back will help to steer him.

Variety

A four-year-old horse can be introduced to poles on the ground, leading on to small grids and courses of jumps. As his muscles develop, correct riding will teach him to work from his hindquarters and eventually to come 'on the bit' – that is, accepting the bit kindly and confidently and not backing off from it. Lessons should be varied in order to maintain interest, and the youngster should gradually be given more to think about and introduced to small competitions to add variety.

Riding young horses

If your riding school gives you a young horse to ride it is a compliment, because they obviously think you are good enough and trust you to cope. It is also a responsibility, because many horses' problems start when they are young, with poor riders, too many different riders, slightly different aids or techniques before they have fully understood what is required. Also, riders who have come off when the horse has expressed his confusion, perhaps by bucking or rearing, can encourage the horse to do this every time he has problems with a rider.

Problems

When riding and training a young horse, you are bound to hit occasional problems. Keep calm and, if necessary, go back a stage. It is vital to have a trainer or someone experienced who can watch you both and help you to work out why things are not going quite right. It is also important that you keep riding well-schooled horses as well as your youngster, so that what you are aiming for remains fresh in your mind.

'Trying it on'

Many trainers say that there comes a point when a young horse will test his rider to see how much he can get away with, or not have to do. Some behavioural therapists say that horses do not think deviously like this, and that this behaviour can be caused by mental or physical distress or discomfort. Whatever the truth, the fact is that there usually does come a time when a youngster starts being 'difficult' and you need persistent insistence to get over it.

You need to be sure that previous good progress is not causing you to take the youngster on too quickly in his training, before he has had time to absorb his current level fully. In this situation, there is the possibility that you are confusing him by perhaps using the kind of finer nuances of aids that would be understood by a more experienced horse but not by your youngster. Also be sure that you are not overdoing things, overlooking an injury, pain or discomfort (which can certainly cause this problem), or mentally or physically pressuring the horse. Expert help sympathetic to the horse is usually well worthwhile.

Riding difficult horses

Difficult horses are usually confused horses, or those who have been abused by poor trainers and riders punishing (usually whipping) the horse for their own failings. Some difficult horses are badly managed – over-fed and under-worked; others are ridden inappropriately for their needs. Some riders also use very harsh bits and bit contact, stabbing the horse in the mouth, spurring him, and tying him up and down with forceful training aids. Eventually, a horse that would have been perfectly amenable if he had been trained correctly and empathetically from the start will become difficult, or even a rogue.

The correct approach

As a client at a riding centre, you should not be exposed to rogue horses, but learning to ride difficult horses is certainly part of your equestrian education. Difficult horses usually demand both quiet firmness and persistent determination. Any mistreatment will set them back instantly to square one. Normally, a good thing to do is take them back to the beginning and consistently train them correctly. The word 'consistent' is key: apart from probably having been brutalized, what they lack is consistent, firm, fair treatment. You will need expert teaching and supervision to turn around a horse like this, although of course some are easier than others.

This horse is about to rear but the rider is making things worse by pulling on his mouth instead of driving him forwards briskly.

The right not to ride

Horses that are difficult to ride, often misbehaving under saddle, can test some riders to their limit and actually put them off the sport of riding altogether. There is no need for this to happen. Never be afraid to tell your riding school or teacher that you are nervous or even frightened of riding a particular horse (especially if it is your own) and really get to the bottom of why. You are well within your rights to refuse to ride him, so do not allow yourself to be pushed into it for any reason.

Finding a freelance teacher

If you buy your own horse, you may need a freelance teacher. There are many freelance teachers, with different training philosophies and you must have one on the same wavelength as you. You may feel that you don't know enough to have a wavelength but you will find that you get on with some teachers and not others and agree with the attitudes of some towards your horse but not others.

Checklist
✓ sources of information
✓ watching a lesson
✓ value of qualifications
✓ costs and insurance

Word of mouth

Usually, the best way to find a suitable teacher is for someone whose opinion you respect to recommend someone. If your friend or acquaintance thinks in broadly the same way you do, it is highly likely that the recommended teacher will, too.

Advertisements

Sometimes freelance teachers advertise in the local, regional or even national equestrian press. Societies subscribing to a particular way of riding will usually publish a journal or newsletter of some kind, which will also probably feature advertisements for teachers specializing in that kind of horse riding.

You may hear a rather cynical view that if a teacher is advertising for work they can't be any good. This is not necessarily so. Freelance work of any kind can be very erratic and most self-employed people experience ups and downs in their workloads. So don't shy off advertisements, but ring up and get details.

Watch a lesson or two

Ask the teacher if you can go along and watch them teach so that you can get an idea of their principles. As most

This horse is walking out well (note the hind leg action) but if the rider sat up a little more, brought his elbows back to his hips and lengthened his reins accordingly, things would be even better.

Insurance

A conscientious teacher should stress that your horse needs to be sound and healthy, with feet and shoes in good condition (not to mention teeth and back), that your tack needs to fit well and be in safe condition, and that you will need to wear a hard hat up to the latest specifications. Apart from being responsible, insurance requirements will probably demand all this – and no responsible teacher would teach without insurance.

freelancers teach on private property, visiting horse owners at their homes or livery yards, this may also involve asking the client or owner if you could watch a lesson. Some will certainly say no, but usually a suitable venue can be arranged and you can watch – in silence – what goes on and listen to the teacher's ideas and advice.

Talk on the telephone

If watching a lesson is not possible, telephone the teacher and tell them about your experience and aims, and of course your horse. Also be sure to ask whether they are fully insured and/or have any qualifications.

The teacher should ask you some basic questions about your riding and the horse's training and management, any problems you are having and what you aim to achieve. They will also probably ask where you ride and keep your horse, and whether you have access to a suitable ground surface (indoor or outdoor).

If it all sounds good so far, book a lesson.

Qualifications

There are differences of opinion about qualifications: there is no doubt that some qualified teachers are very poor at teaching and some unqualified ones are wonderful. It is also the case that talented, successful riders and horse trainers often cannot teach people effectively because they either do not know what they do instinctively, cannot assess problems when they see a horse and rider in front of them, or cannot express themselves clearly. Some prefer to get on your horse and school him for long periods rather than actually teaching you. This may be fine in some circumstances but you need to be taught as well.

A good teacher will always be happy to discuss queries or problems with you and answer any questions. So if you don't understand something, ask.

Cost

If a teacher seems to be what you are looking for, ask how much they charge. If the fee is fairly high, remember that one good lesson a month (if that is all you can afford) is better than a cheap, poor one every week.

A good, professional teacher will be able to give you a plan of work to keep you going for the forthcoming fortnight or month, until your next lesson, and should be willing to talk through any problems in the meantime on the phone free of charge – provided you don't talk for too long.

ADVANCED RIDING

It is said that the better you are at something the more you enjoy it. Riding is always risky, so the better you do it presumably the safer you will be! Even if you never reach international standard yourself, you can learn a lot from studying your favourite sport at high level and learning to assess the riders' performances. Studying the horses is even more enlightening. You should soon learn which horses are well ridden and are enjoying themselves, and which, despite competing at this level, are not ridden well (from the point of view of humane, logical technique) and are not enjoying it as much as others.

Western sports

Western riding is a sport on its own and there are several different disciplines. It stems from the European classical school and was taken to the Americas by the conquistadors and early settlers. Californian Western riding is possibly now the closest to the original parade and stock-herding seat of the early settlers. Many people unfamiliar with Western riding think first of rodeo riding, but there are other aspects.

Checklist
✓ rodeo events
✓ origins in ranching skills
✓ show riding

Calf-roping

This is one of the five standard events staged at rodeos that have their origins in ranch work. It is a basic test of a cowboy's skill, demanding a well-trained horse and great dexterity with a lasso.

The idea is to rope, then tie, a calf, as if to prepare it for branding. The calf is given a start of several seconds down the arena before horse and rider gallop in headlong pursuit. When the cowboy is in the right position, he tosses his lasso over the calf's head and secures the other end of the rope around his saddle horn, throws himself from the saddle while the horse steps back to keep the rope taut, and runs towards the calf. The cowboy flips the calf on to its side and ties three of its legs together with a length of rope he has been holding between his teeth.

Time is the deciding factor for the winner, although a cowboy will be disqualified if the calf slips out of the tie within five seconds.

Calf-roping in action. Many Western horses, particularly those of the Quarter Horse breed, are noted for their 'cow savvy', seeming instinctively to know how to herd and cope with cattle.

the rear part of the saddle on the right side and below the horse's belly, buckling to the nearside point strap.

There is obviously only one stirrup, on the left side.

Saddling up

1 Carry the saddle with your right hand, holding the fixed head and the lining down your hip and thigh. The girth and balance strap can be attached on the left side and held, with the flap strap, in your left hand.

2 Place the saddle carefully on the horse's back a little too far forward and slide it back.

3 Buckle the balance strap to the point strap, and the girth to the first two girth straps. Fasten the girth on the right side. The balance strap lies on top of the girth and must not be tighter than the girth. The flap strap should be fastened no tighter than the girth and balance strap.

Ideally, two people should saddle up the horse – one to hold the saddle in place and the other to move around the horse carrying out the various steps. The girth and balance strap are finally adjusted on the right side once the rider is mounted. It is crucial not to have the balance strap too far back or too tight, as this will cause some horses to buck.

Showing classes

Classes available to side-saddle riders may include equitation classes, working hunter, showjumping, turnout,

dressage, ladies
children's ponies

Horses for sid

The good side-sa
and shoulder, ar
suitable conform
trained to carry a
bridle can be us
even with its lac
distribution. The
days, so his stint

Riding side-s

The rider has a l
astride in the no
then bring the ri
the rider must a
saddle but with t
the left heel an
(except possibly
encourages the r
balance and the

The seat of th
The unusual sen
be disconcerting

Rodeos

Larger rodeos feature other events as well as the standard ones. In cutting horse classes the horse is trained to separate a calf or steer from a herd, and then place itself between the animal and its herd to prevent its return. Another is team roping involving two cowboys, one of whom lassoes a calf around the head while his partner ropes its hindlegs. There are also chuck-wagon races and barrel racing.

Saddle-bronc riding

The second standard rodeo event is saddle-bronc riding, which evokes memories of the method used by cowboys to break their mounts for riding. The saddle is a modified stock saddle (smaller and with no front horn), while the rein is merely a rope attached to the horse's halter. A bucking strap is tightened around the horse's flanks to encourage it to buck. The horses are chosen by lottery and are specialist bucking horses.

The horses leave the special chute in which the cowboy mounts, bucking wildly. The ride must last ten seconds and calls for extraordinary balance and timing to achieve maximum scores.

Other standard rodeo events

The three remaining standard events arose from cowboys bragging that they were tough enough to ride a bronc bareback, stay aboard a brahma bull or wrestle a steer to the ground.

Although **bareback bronc riding** certainly requires brute strength, the rider can use only one hand to hold the grip attached to a strap around the horse's girth. In this sport, the ride limit is eight seconds.

Bull riding is particularly perilous, because the bull will chase and try to gore an unseated cowboy. The rider can use both hands on the girth grip and, again, must stay on board for eight seconds.

In **steer wrestling**, a cowboy gallops after a steer with another rider racing on the other side to keep the animal straight. The cowboy flings himself from the saddle and grabs the steer's horns, planting his boots in the dirt to achieve a firm grip. He then wrestles it on to its side. The quickest competitor wins.

Saddle-bronc riding is a dangerous sport in which bad falls and injuries are to be expected. Even the best riders must stay on for only ten seconds.

Western-style show riding

Stock-seat equitation Contestants are judged on their riding skills and their horse's performance at walk, jog (trot) and lope (canter), sometimes also performing movements such as figures of eight and the impressive sliding stops.

Reining The Western equivalent of a dressage test, including figures of eight, turns on the forehand and haunches, and halts, this class tests the qualities needed for ranch work.

Trail horse The horses negotiate obstacles that might be found on a cross-country ride.

Pleasure horse The horses are shown at walk, jog and lope to demonstrate their suitability as Western hacks.

Side-saddle riding

Side-saddle riding evokes the elegance of bygone days. It is a thriving aspect of show riding and is still seen out hunting. Men ride side saddle sometimes, often because it does not demand the spread of the hip joints and is suitable for riders with arthritic hips or other disabilities that make astride riding difficult or painful. There is a variety of showing classes for children and adults, on the flat and over jumps.

Checklist
✓ deve
✓ the
✓ the
✓ side

These two ladies with
lovely picture, in a sic

The moder

The modern
former desig
that the rider

The tree i
cast iron. Th
fixed head,
left. The low
tree and can
or to accom

The seat
balance. Iml
give the hors
leave a clear
the tree poin
nor must th
saddle flap
horse's shou
the bottom
smaller righ

There ar
normally sh
third one –
the vertical
strap called

History

Probably the heyday of side-saddle riding for practical and general purposes was during the 19th century in England and Ireland. As early as the 5th century BC, paintings and carvings show women sitting sideways with their legs dangling down the horse's right side.

A type of side-saddle was used in England around the mid-12th century, although women certainly rode astride before this. The modern side-saddle with pommels was introduced around 1500 by Catherine de Medici. Designs continued to emerge, culminating in the current pattern in the early 20th century to accommodate the new forward type of riding out hunting.

Dressage

Dressage is a popular sport in which anyone can compete from a basic level. There is no jumping involved and certainly the lower-level competitions ask the horse and rider only to walk, trot and canter (the three basic gaits) on straight lines, around corners and on large circles. The competition takes the form of tests designed to examine the level of training and ability of each horse-and-rider combination.

Checklist
✓ a system of tests
✓ required movements
✓ what judges look for
✓ the right horse

Levels of difficulty

The lowest-level dressage tests are called Preliminary in the UK and Training level in the United States. Tests rise in difficulty up to the most difficult, the Grand Prix.

At higher levels, horses must perform a number of more advanced movements:

Lateral work moving diagonally sideways in the three gaits to show suppleness and obedience.

Pirouettes in canter may be required – here, the forelegs move in a circle around the hindlegs, which move in a much smaller circle.

Two flamboyant kinds of trot may also be required:

Passage a lofty, slow trot in which the horse springs proudly, lifting his legs higher than normal in a well-marked rhythm.

Piaffe in which the horse does the same thing but on the spot, barely moving forward at all.

The test

The horse and rider move around an arena of a set size, 40 x 20 m (130 x 65 ft) or 60 x 20 m (197 x 65 ft), on the edges of which are displayed letters or 'markers'. The larger size is used for international competitions, to allow room for the more complex tests and because of the longer distances over which the horse is required to extend his gaits. However, 'lesser' competitions now sometimes use the larger arena, although the smaller one is standard for most establishments and competitions.

A knowledgeable horseperson can tell from the type of muscle development whether or not that horse has been correctly trained.

The rider obtains a test sheet for the competition they are entering, which states what movements must be performed between which markers and in what order. The judges look for flowing movement, good balance, rhythm and obedience from the horse, and tactful, sympathetic technique from the rider. Accuracy (doing the movements where the test stipulates) is important. At higher levels, the horse needs to show personality and a certain panache in his performance.

Horses for dressage

Most specialized dressage horses today are warmbloods, a type that originated on mainland Europe, where each region of each country often had its own native type of horse. These were mainly 'cold-blooded', physically heavy horses with placid natures used for farming work and transport such as coaches and carriages.

To produce the lighter, elegant horses needed for riding and competition, 'hot-blooded' English Thoroughbred horses were imported and bred with local heavy horses. The Thoroughbred often has a fiery nature, is lightly but strongly built, and is very courageous. Mixed with heavier horses, it has produced the now-famous 'warm-blooded' breeds, which excel at dressage and also showjumping. Some Arabian blood has also been introduced for style, stamina and a more equable temperament.

'Dressage' is a French word meaning to put the finishing touches to something. It does not simply mean 'training' as many people think.

Frequently asked questions

Q What do the judges look for in a horse/rider pair in competition?

A The main things are accuracy of the school figures or patterns and correctness of the horse's gaits. There are other things such as obedience, and presence or personality (the 'look at me' factor), which is 'unofficial' but influences the judges, who are only human after all. Certainly at the higher levels, specific presentation and clothing (turnout) is a requirement.

Q I do not have an expensive warmblood. Can I still compete in dressage?

A Certainly. Any healthy, sound horse that moves well has a good chance of winning a rosette at lower levels if he is ridden correctly. Willingness and accuracy are the primary qualities looked for at lower levels, so the horse's breed is not that important. An element of 'lift' or spring in the gaits always helps.

Dressage is a strenuous activity for the horse, akin to gymnastics in humans. The training makes the horses strong and agile.

HEALTH CARE

In the General Care section of this book, we said that the aspect of horse ownership that best ensures good health is correct care and management appropriate to the horse concerned. There are times, though, when even the best of care fails to keep your horse healthy. Any horse can become ill if the circumstances are right, any horse can become infested with parasites, be injured and, of course, need regular attention to teeth and feet plus vaccinations and an annual health check. Your veterinary surgeon is your greatest ally here (always have veterinary fees insurance), although other health care professionals may also be able to help in their specialized ways.

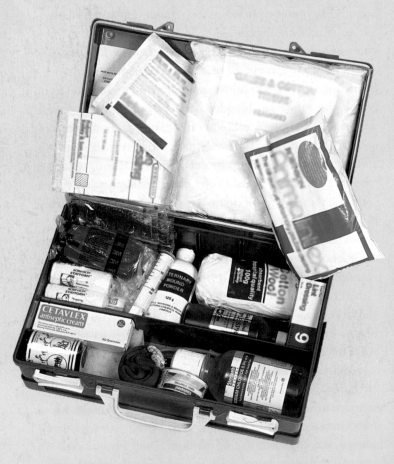

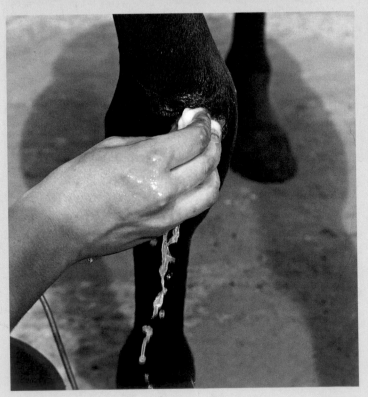

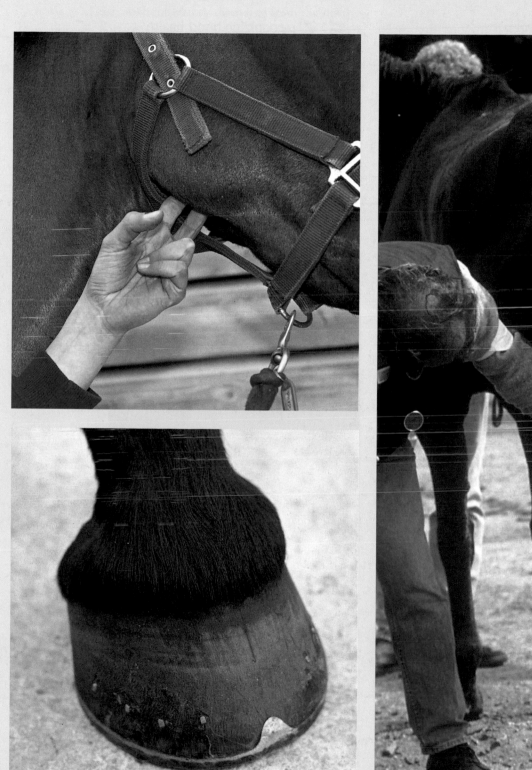

INDEX

ACKNOWLEDGEMENTS

Executive Editor Trevor Davies
Editor Emma Pattison
Executive Art Editor Leigh Jones
Designer Patrick McLeavey
Picture Research Sophie Delpech,
Vickie Walters
Production Controller Nosheen Shan

Photographic Acknowledgements in Source Order

Ardea 8 bottom left, 11 bottom left, 13 top; /Liz Bomford 14; /John Daniels 5 top left, 31, 50, 167, 187 bottom; /Jean-Marc La-Roque 16; /M. Warson 40.
Bob Langrish 2-3, 5 top right, 5 bottom left, 7 bottom, 8 top, 9 top, 9 bottom, 10, 13 bottom right, 15 centre right, 15 bottom left, 17, 19 top right, 21, 23 top left, 23 top right, 29 top right, 29 bottom left, 39 top right, 39 centre right, 45 top left, 56, 61 top left, 65, 68, 69, 78, 79, 87, 105, 108 bottom right, 130, 132, 133, 138, 139, 147, 154 top right, 154 bottom right, 154 bottom left, 155 top, 155 bottom, 156, 157, 158, 160, 161, 162, 163, 164, 165 top, 165 bottom, 168, 170, 171, 172, 173, 174, 175, 176, 177, 178 bottom right, 179 bottom left, 182, 187 top left, 188, 189.
Houghton's Horses/Kit Houghton 7 top, 19 bottom left, 37, 41, 64, 75, 91, 97, 159, 166, 169, 179 right, 184.
Octopus Publishing Group Limited/Vincent Oliver 1, 6 bottom left, 22 top left, 32, 33, 38, 42, 45 bottom left, 47 bottom, 57, 62, 76, 77, 81 top left, 81 centre left, 81 top right, 81 centre right; /Bob Atkins 106, 107 top left; /Equestrian Photographic Services Ltd 99; /Kit Houghton 6 top right, 22 bottom, 30, 43, 44 bottom right, 49 top, 49 bottom, 55, 60 top right, 60 bottom right, 61 top right, 61 bottom, 63, 66, 67, 70, 71 left, 71 right, 73 top, 73 centre, 88 left, 88 centre right, 88 bottom right, 96, 101 top right, 101 top left, 101 centre left, 101 centre right, 101 bottom left, 102, 104, 107 bottom right, 108 bottom left, 109 top left, 113, 115, 136, 141, 150, 178 bottom left, 179 top left, 181, 183; /Alyson M. Kyles 48; /Bob Langrish 5 centre left, 5 bottom right, 5 bottom centre right, 5 top centre right, 8 bottom right, 11 top right, 20, 44 top right, 44 bottom left, 45 right, 46, 51, 52, 53, 54, 58, 59, 60 left, 82, 83 top right, 83 top left, 83 bottom left, 84 left, 84 right, 85, 86, 90, 92, 93 left, 93 right, 94 top left, 94 bottom right, 98, 103, 108 top, 109 right, 109 bottom right, 111 left, 111 right, 112, 114, 117 top left, 117 top right, 117 bottom right, 117 bottom left, 118 top left, 118 top right, 118 bottom right, 118 bottom left, 120, 121, 122 left, 122 right, 123 left, 123 right, 124 left, 124 right, 126 left, 126 right, 127 left, 127 right, 128, 129, 131, 134, 135, 137, 140, 142, 143 left, 143 right, 143 centre, 144, 145, 146, 148, 149, 151, 152, 153, 178 top left, 180; /John Rigby 47 top.